Christmas in County Cork

Rescued Folklore and History from
Ireland's southernmost county

Mike Baldwin

First published in Great Britain in 2025

ISBN: 978-1-0369-7412-1

Copyright © Mike Baldwin, 2025
www.mike-baldwin.net

Cover illustration by the author.

All rights reserved. No part of this publication may be reproduced, stored in a retrieval system, or transmitted in any form or by any means, electronic, mechanical, photocopying, recording, or otherwise, without the prior permission of both the copyright owner and the above publisher.

Some of the texts in this book are transcribed from the School's Collection with the kind permission of the National Folklore Commission, University College Dublin. https://www.duchas.ie/en

For Jimmy Downey, a true Christian man, whose humour, kindness, and quiet counsel enriched so many lives.

St Patrick's Bridge, from S. C. Hall, *Ireland: Its Scenery, Character*, vol. 1 (London: How and Parsons, 1841).

Contents

Figures	8
Foreword	9
Prologue - A Candle at the Edge of the World	11
Darkness and Light	27
When the Sea Came for Christmas	44
Memory	61
Faith and Superstition	77
Traditions	95
Winter Weather	127
The Origins of Christmas in Ireland	140
Commerce in Cork	146
Rupture	157
A State is Born - Christmas 1922 in Cork	163
Conclusion	166
Bibliography	182
Index	184

Figures

Figure 1. Map of County Cork. 13
Figure 2. Bantry Bay in snow. 17
Figure 3. Panoramic of Cork City, 1750. 24
Figure 4. Nottingham Evening Post, 21 July 1900. 39
Figure 5. Manchester Courier, 12 December 1900. 39
Figure 6. Runcorn Guardian, 16 January 1901. 40
Figure 7. Panoramic of Kinsale in 1750. 46
Figure 8. Panoramic of Youghal in 1750. 50
Figure 9. Entrance to Cork Harbour. 53
Figure 10. The Wren Boys. 104
Figure 11. The Cove of Cobh. 109
Figure 12. Map of Cork City. 148
Figure 13. The Corn Exchange, Cork. 151
Figure 14. The Cork Herald, 24 December 1859. 152
Figure 15. Cork Constitution, 24 December 1860. 153
Figure 16. Cork Constitution, 24 December 1870. 154
Figure 17. Cork Daily Herald, 24 December 1870. 154
Figure 18. Cork Examiner, 29 December 1847. 174

Foreword

A Very Mizen Christmas

Kathleen Downey

Christmas was not mentioned in our house until after the 8th of December, And I remember a week before Christmas, climbing walls of the ruins of the old Famine houses in search of ivy. We used it to decorate pictures and the shelves. And streamers were tacked to the ceiling. On the 8th of December, and the Sunday after, a big parish concert was held in the hall on two nights. This was to raise funds for coal for the school. Local singers of any age from Goleen school sang in groups of two or three. There was also a three-act play. At the time, there were a lot more local people in the locality. A queue the length of North Street went to see it.

Everything was family orientated, neighbours interacted, and generations mixed. The festive season was home time when farmers did no heavy work. They fed the pigs and hens and milked the cows, but there was no sowing of crops that week. What brought in the Christmas was getting a good price for turkeys. A buyer would come to the crossroads to meet the farmer and could buy up to twenty.

On Christmas Eve, the youngest in the house lit the candle. This was a present from the grocery. I recall a hole was carved in a turnip and either a red or white candle inserted. And it would be left lighting all night. Small candles were placed in every window.

It was dark outside by 6pm. That was the time for the coming of Santa. We got books like Jack in The Beanstalk. Presents were found in the stockings by the fireplace. Afterwards, two elderly neighbours would call scíorting. It was a social with tea and cake. They called to see what we had got. Toys like a car or doll, an orange or a bar of chocolate, as well as crayons or a fountain pen. Everybody was in bed by 10pm to be up for mass at 7am.

We walked the three miles to mass. Light was in every house along the way. Christmas dinner was not important. I can't remember it. But I do have memories of neighbours calling on Christmas night for tea, a chat and singing old ballads like Homes of Donegal. And news of local happenings was shared.

On St Stephen's night, the Wren Ball was a big night out. This was a dance at the parish hall with a band from 9pm until 2am. There was dancing, singing and music. It was time to see those working in England, home for Christmas. There was a mineral bar in the hall, and only a mineral bar for everyone from 16 years to 60 years old. I enjoyed dancing all night. Waltzes, quick step, fox trot and a half set. This was big in rural areas. As was the new dress for the occasion. A lot of these came from America.

Emigration was high at the time. The American relatives sent a parcel or two at Christmas. They saw want, they sent home to help and were very good to home. The excitement was great when the postman brought them on the carrier of his bicycle. Usually, there would be bits for Christmas, but my mother robbed the parcel before we would see it. They would always send a letter about their family in a Christmas card. A parcel weighed about a stone. It came in a cotton flour bag that was sewn, so there was no danger of it bursting in transit. It consisted mostly of clothes: dresses, jumpers, shoes, scarves, and coats. These were for anyone in the family they would fit and no one in particular. However, it was always great to get tea, because tea was scarce at the time.

Christmas brought tradition, family life and communicating with people. It was a time of celebration and we looked forward to it.

First published in The Southern Star, 25th December 2003

Prologue - A Candle at the Edge of the World

The first light in the valley was not the sun, but a candle. Long before dawn, while the hills above Drimoleague were still wrapped in mist and frost, a woman, her shawl drawn tight around her, lit a taper from the embers of the previous night's fire, shielding it from the draught that crept beneath the thatch. It caught, and she pressed the flame to a short stub of beeswax, and a thin, trembling light flickered into life on the windowsill of the cottage. Its glow reflected in her eyes, tired, yes, but steadfast, as she whispered a prayer for those far from home.

Outside, the air was still. Cold clung to the earth, and the stone walls of the cabin shimmered with a silver breath. Inside, her children slept, curled together under threadbare blankets, limbs tangled, dreams unspoken. The man of the house stirred on the settle. Soon he would tend to the cattle. The frost lay deep. The days were short. But this was Christmas morning, and the candle had been lit. It was a ritual older than memory. The candle in the window was lit to welcome the Holy Family, but also to signal to neighbours, to spirits, to anyone watching that this house was not lost to despair. It was a light for the Christ child. But it was also a light for those far from home: a son in Boston, a daughter in service in London.

In Catholic Ireland, the home was a place of prayer as much as the chapel. The domestic rituals of Christmastide were suffused with spirituality, particularly where access to clergy or sacraments might be irregular. The home became the church, the table the altar, the candle the vigil, the shared meal the Eucharist.

Women in particular carried these customs. They passed down prayers, hymns, and traditions, not formally, but through rhythm, repetition, and presence. Their work was devotional as well as domestic. As one oral tradition from the Schools' Collection notes, 'Twas the woman who set the holy table on Christmas Eve, with three white loaves and a light for each soul gone before.' And yet, theirs is a quiet authorship. Historians have only recently begun to fully acknowledge the cultural labour of Irish women in preserving ritual life through famine, exile, and colonisation. In Christmas, their role was central: lighting candles, preparing votives, teaching carols in Irish, telling the Nativity as part of family lore, not as story but as an inheritance.

On this morning, the woman began to hum. The melody was older than English, sung softly in the native tongue.

> *Don Oíche úd i mBeithil*
> *Beidh solas 's sonas ann…*
> *On that night in Bethlehem*
> *There will be light and joy…*

The carol did not need accompaniment. The fire was music enough. When the youngest child stirred, the mother would sing it again, this time with arms around shoulders, voice warming with memory. For these Irish carols held theological weight and cultural defiance. They spoke not only of Christ's birth but of kinship, survival, and longing. The journey to Mass could be treacherous. The path wound through hills slick with frost, and the church, a simple whitewashed building, had no heating. But it had a bell. And candles. And the Latin would rise like mist to the rafters, the Irish remained murmured beneath breath.

There, they might see neighbours not spoken to since All Souls. They might pray for the departed whose names were not written in any parish register but kept in their hearts. The priest would speak of light in darkness, of the child born poor, of the manger and its straw.

It is easy and tempting for modern observers to cast these rural Christmases in terms of lack. There were no crackers or confections, no garlands or wrapping paper. But to frame these experiences solely by what they didn't have is to miss what they did: intention, community, collective rhythm.

In pre-Famine Ireland, the material world was scarce, but the symbolic world was rich. Anthropologists and historians alike have shown that oral culture and domestic ritual were central to Irish identity during this period. Christmas was a convergence point: where the liturgical calendar, the agricultural cycle, and the kinship network intersected. That candle in the window, then, is not quaint nostalgia.

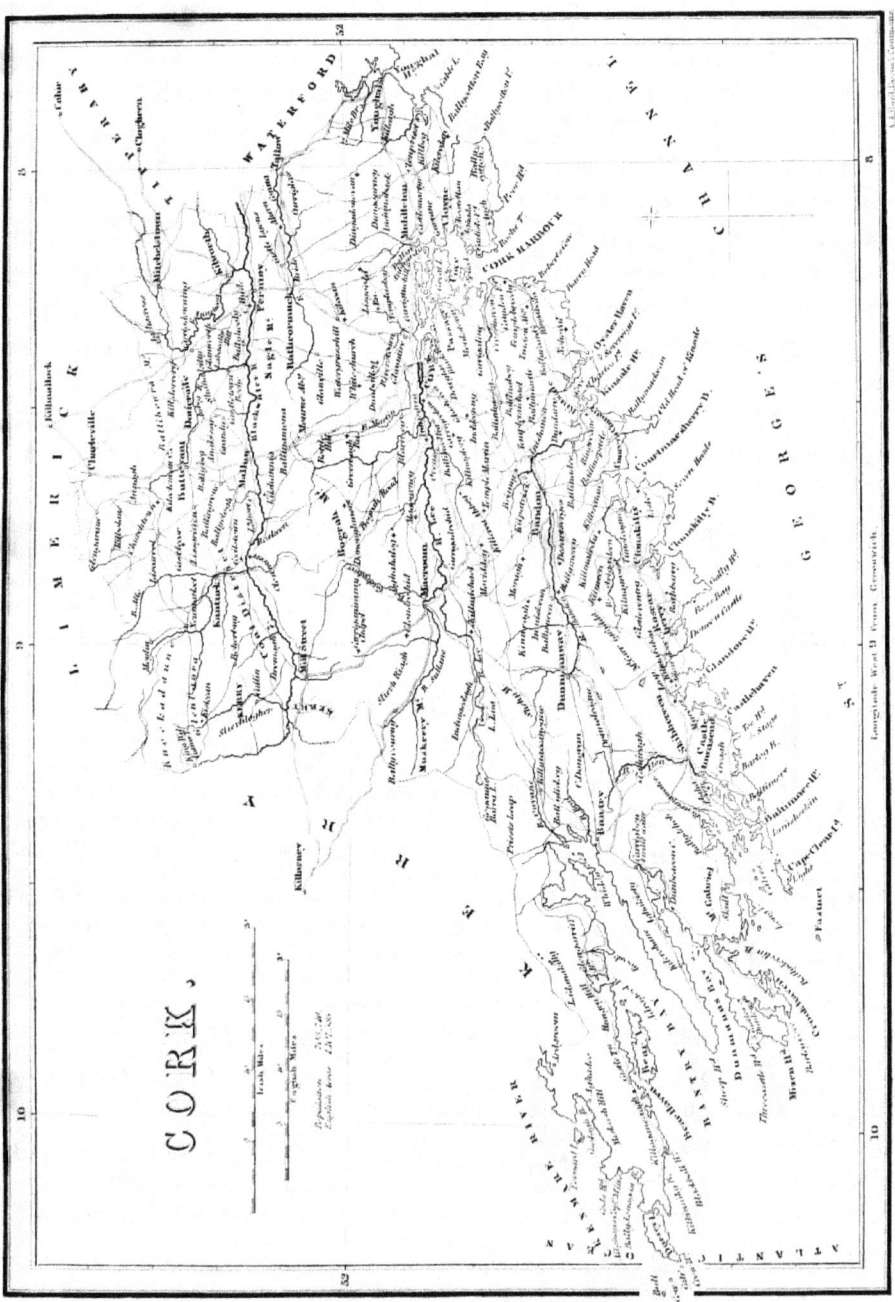

Figure 1, County Cork, S. C. Hall, Ireland: Its Scenery and Character, vol. 1 (London: How, 1846).

It is theology, folklore, and social memory combined. It says: *We are still here. We remember. We believe.*

For the people of rural Cork in the early nineteenth century, Christmas was not a holiday of spectacle or gift-giving. It was sacred, domestic, and profoundly communal, a series of gestures that turned the ordinary into the divine. A sprig of holly above the hearth. A boiled pudding carefully wrapped in muslin. A pot of cream, set aside from the cow's milking, if the animal was still well. The men might shave, the children might wash with warmed well-water. But the true preparation was of the soul: confession, reconciliation, the quiet lighting of a candle in the dark.

Far from this windswept homestead, Christmas took another form entirely. In the drawing rooms of Cork's great houses, candlelight met candelabras. Violins replaced tin whistles. Goose was carved beneath gilded ceilings while, outside, the land began to hunger.

And so, we leave the stone cottage, its light still burning, and journey now to Bantry House, where the season unfolded with elegance and plenty.

Christmas at Bantry House

At Bantry House, nestled on the wooded slope above the bay, Christmas arrived not with want, but with orchestration. The house was dressed in silence and splendour. The air smelled of beeswax, oranges, and coal smoke; garlands of ivy and fir hung from the staircases; silver gleamed in the candlelight. In the drawing room, the harp had been tuned. Servants moved briskly but softly; their footfalls muffled on Turkish rugs. A fire hissed in the grate as dusk fell on Christmas Eve, and from the far side of the water, gulls called above the quiet waves.

It was 1848, and inside this great Georgian villa, seat of the Earls of Bantry, the festivities were carefully prepared. The guest rooms were full, and the table laid. Yet despite the soft laughter and clink of glasses, something else pulsed beneath the surface: a tension, barely spoken, that stretched beyond the tall windows and into the hills beyond. For this was the fourth Christmas of the Great Famine. And Bantry was not immune to its shadow.

Bantry House was not only a private residence, it was a declaration of status, refinement, and imperial connectivity. The library housed rare volumes from the Continent. The furniture bore the curves of French craftsmanship. Italian tapestries, brought back from Grand Tours, hung in the stairwell. Even the Christmas trimmings bore the signature of the global: dried figs from Smyrna, crystal decanters from Bohemia, a Norfolk goose glazed with Madeira wine.

For the Anglo-Irish gentry, such seasonal displays were status-affirming, signs of civility, culture, and continuity in a land increasingly resistant to their presence. The rituals of a Victorian Christmas, introduced with enthusiasm from England and often performed with theatrical intensity, allowed the elite to stage a version of belonging, to inhabit an identity that was both Irish and not. The music might include an Irish air, but only if arranged for quartet.

And yet, even as the guests gathered for the Christmas meal in Bantry House's great dining room, some could not keep their minds from what lay beyond the estate walls.

The roads beyond Bantry House were heavy with mud and grief. In Skibbereen, less than a day's ride away, mass graves were filling. In the villages along Bantry Bay, famine cabins clung to the earth like broken teeth. Across Ireland, an estimated one million had already died; another million were in flight. The Earl himself had toured some of the worst-affected areas. Now, seated at the head of a table laden with delicacies, the Earl of Bantry toyed with his wineglass. Conversation turned to politics. A guest mentioned Lord Clarendon's latest speech on relief. Another murmured about disturbances in West Cork, by which they meant hungry people begging with more insistence than was polite. A few guests lowered their eyes.

Earlier that afternoon, the estate's chaplain had preached a Christmas sermon in the private chapel. The message had been eloquent and well-measured: compassion, dignity, the gift of grace. He had spoken of the light of Christ shining in dark times and called on his congregation to remember the poor with both purse and prayer. A basket of donations had been collected, coins, clothing, food. But no one spoke of it now. The Anglo-Irish relationship with Christmas charity was a complex and often contradictory one. On the one hand, many landowners saw themselves as benevolent stewards, morally obligated to offer relief in hard times. Estate records from this period often include references to alms, school dinners, or coal deliveries. On the other hand, these gestures were rarely free from the desire for social control. Charity was a tool, of conscience, of political leverage, and of paternalism.

At Bantry House, the charity box sat beside a bowl of sugared almonds. Guests gave, as they always did, but the giving was part of the script, alongside the toasts, the music, and the rich food. The social season required spectacle. And to express compassion through Christmas rituals allowed the elite to maintain both power and moral superiority. Yet this moral world was fraying. The Famine had laid bare the limits of estate benevolence. Political radicals called it genocide. Priests decried the inaction of landlords from pulpits.

Even the British press, at times, was scathing. Against this backdrop, the well-appointed Christmas table could feel like an accusation.

In staging Christmas, the Anglo-Irish elite were not only hosting, they were defining the parameters of Irish festivity. Their Christmas was one of parlour games, imported traditions, and Protestant liturgy, O Come, All Ye Faithful in full harmonies, Lessons and Carols in candlelit chapels. But their celebration also existed in tension with older Irish customs. In town and country, the local Catholic families were preparing for Midnight Mass. There would be candles in their windows too, but not from chandeliers. Their hymns would be in Irish, their food boiled and shared. They might pass Bantry House on the way to the chapel, walking, silent and reverent, their faces unreadable as they glimpsed the light and sound within. By midnight, the guests at Bantry House would be raising glasses of claret. The fire would be banked. A young cousin might recite a seasonal poem, something by Wordsworth or Moore. Laughter would rise again. But somewhere in the shadows of that great house, a servant might pause - might recall her own family, lighting a candle in a cottage up the Beara.

Not far from this ballroom of soft candlelight, the town of Skibbereen lay blanketed not in snow, but in silence and grief. There, the birth of Christ was not marked by finery or fanfare, but by the rattle of fever carts, the rustle of straw beds, and the flicker of votive candles lit not for joy, but for the dying.

Skibbereen, Christmas 1847

In Skibbereen, Christmas arrived not with carols, but with hunger. Not with cheer, but with silence, thick and leaden, like the smoke that drifted from the fever sheds at the edge of the parish. The past few years had carved deep hollows in the town. The streets were wet with sleet, though snow rarely held long this far south. A single bell tolled, its sound swallowed by mist and grief. Inside a thatched cabin on the edge of town, a mother set a candle in the window, not out of hope, but from habit or memory. Or the aching wish that some light might still answer the darkness. She might whisper a prayer as she passed the nursery door. For Christmas, even here, was never just an English import. It was layered, with guilt, grace, ritual, and memory.

Figure 2. Bantry Bay in snow. After Hall (1847).

It was December 1847: Black '47, the grimmest winter of the Great Famine. The potatoes had failed again. The workhouses were full. Soup kitchens had begun to shut due to lack of funds. Children wrapped in torn shawls stood barefoot at the gates of the Poor Law Guardians, begging for broth. Parish priests buried dozens each week, a few in coffins, most simply shrouded. Emaciated men collapsed outside churches. Women laboured not for pay but for a ladle of gruel. Christmas, if it came at all, passed over Skibbereen like a ghost.

Inside the cabin, a girl lay in a heap of straw, too weak to sit. Her cheeks were sunken, her eyes fixed on the flicker of light in the window. Her mother knelt by the hearth, stirring a pot of thin nettle broth. There was no meat, no pudding, no Mass. The priest had passed through earlier that day, leaving behind the sacrament and a blessing, and perhaps a tear he thought no one saw.

On a wooden board, the mother had arranged a few pebbles in a circle; a crude nativity, a reminder that God too was born in poverty. She sang softly in Irish, her voice breaking:

Dia do bheatha, a Naí Íosa...
Welcome, Holy Child of Jesus.

There were no visitors. There was no table laid. But the candle still burned.

Skibbereen became a symbol of national anguish during the Famine, the name itself invoked in ballads, editorials, and appeals across Ireland and Britain. Reporters from London, Cork, and Dublin travelled to its lanes to witness the devastation. What they found appalled even the most hardened. A letter published in the *Cork Examiner* told of 'families dying side by side in ditches... children with nothing to wear but rags.' Another described 'the odour of death mingling with the smell of peat smoke,' as funerals passed by with no prayers, only a nod from the gravedigger and the thud of clay.

Christmas could not escape the wider reality. Some relief committees tried to provide extra rations. Churches in Cork city organised charity boxes for 'the most afflicted of the western baronies.' But the aid was scattered and insufficient – their congregations were starving too. The British government's policies, reluctant, delayed, often punitive, were felt most acutely here.

Even as English markets bustled with yuletide goods, the quays of Cork exported grain and cattle. In Skibbereen, people died within the sight of food being loaded onto ships for transportation to the British mainland.

And yet, the season still held its place. Midnight Mass was celebrated in whatever chapels could bear it. People walked miles through freezing rain to kneel together in sorrow and solidarity. Priests, like Fr Nicholas O'Connor, who served in the Skibbereen region, wrote impassioned letters to the press, not only seeking aid, but reminding the world that even in devastation, the people believed. The rituals were pared down, but not erased. A rosary said beside a dying child. A Christmas hymn whispered under breath. The tradition of lighting a candle in the window took on a new meaning: it became not only a symbol of welcome but of witness, a protest against the darkness, a flame for the dead.

In Irish folk culture, Christmas had always been more than festivity, it was a hinge in the year, a time when the veil between the living and the lost grew thin. The Famine heightened this instinct. Ethnographers have argued that trauma in Irish communities was often processed through ritual: repetition, music, candlelight, naming. Christmas became one such frame, a time to make absence visible, to fold grief into faith.

Theologically, the season's messages of hope, birth, and divine presence in poverty resonated in powerful and painful ways. Clergy invoked the Nativity not as a quaint tableau but as a radical promise: *Christ was born into hunger, cold, rejection. He is with you now.* That spiritual defiance would echo in later Irish memory. In oral testimonies, Christmas during the Famine is rarely described in terms of what was eaten or done. Instead, it is remembered for what was felt: sorrow, solidarity, reverence.

Some families in Skibbereen received letters in December from sons and daughters gone abroad, to Boston, Liverpool, Quebec. The letters often carried shillings, handkerchiefs, sometimes a holy card or a small mirror. To those in this famine-ravished town they were bitter-sweet.

> We will have roast fowl and apples for Christmas. But I light the candle here in Boston for Da, and say the same prayer I heard in Shronell. The priest here is from Galway. He sings Mass like at home. I think of you all with every bell.

These letters, read aloud, kept in drawers, or tucked into prayer books, were lifelines. They reminded the people of Skibbereen that they were not forgotten, that somewhere in the world, the Irish were surviving, even thriving. And they bore with them the emotional freight of Christmas: reunion, longing, continuity.

More than any sermon or feast, it was the candle that held the season together. In Skibbereen, in 1847, a lit candle said: We still remember. We still believe. We are still alive. Placed in the window at dusk on Christmas Eve, the candle served multiple functions: it welcomed the Holy Family, it remembered the emigrant, and it honoured the dead. In a context where death was omnipresent, the act of lighting a candle became sacred resistance.

Skibbereen, in 1847, teaches us that Christmas can exist even amid ruin, not in decoration or delight, but in determination. In a mother's whispered hymn. In a child's dying breath. In a candle left burning for no one in particular, and for everyone who is gone.

But while the countryside shuddered under the weight of hunger and loss, another kind of Christmas unfolded in the heart of Cork City.

A Shopfront on Patrick Street

On Patrick Street, or 'Pana,' as the locals call it, December's evenings pulsed with a quiet magic. For those who could afford it, the shop windows gleamed like lanterns in the early dusk. Lamps burned behind drapery displays and perfumed counters. Fir branches drooped gently over polished glass, and holly crowns framed miniature tableaux. Beyond the windows, crowds passed in wool coats and shawls, breath rising in mist. Children pressed noses to the glass. Laughter and music curled like ribbon through the cold air.

It was Christmas in the city, and for many, this was where the season truly began, not at the altar or the hearth, but here, in the golden theatre of the shopfront.

Inside the grand department store, Cash & Co. seventeen-year-old Tom stood stiffly behind a mahogany counter, hands red from the cold and from polishing silver frames. It was his first Christmas in paid work, and the bustle of customers, the ring of the till, the scent of cinnamon soap and damp wool overwhelmed him. He'd been taught to smile, to bow slightly, to wrap parcels with blue ribbon. Some women asked for lace, others for scent. The gentlemen bought gloves. The children stared.

Tom's own Christmas would be simple, a plum cake, perhaps, and a wool scarf if his mother managed to finish knitting it before the big day. But here, in this palace of mirrored walls and velvet-lined boxes, he moved through a different world. For a moment each day, he would glance at the window display, a miniature nativity scene beside a sleigh on artificial snow, and imagine himself one of the figures: noticed, still, warm.

By the late 1800s, retail had become central to the urban Irish Christmas, particularly in cities like Cork. Inspired by British and continental models, Irish merchants transformed December into a spectacle of light, luxury, and aspiration. Shop windows became artistic productions. Advertisements in the *Cork Constitution* and *Examiner* promised *'French gloves, German harmonicas, and the latest goods from the Arcades of London.'* Urban families, especially the growing Catholic middle class, strolled beneath the lamps, admiring the displays, choosing presents with care, even when funds were tight.

This transformation marked a cultural shift. Christmas, once rooted primarily in religious observance and rural folk ritual, now expanded to include consumer experience, visual enchantment, and public performance. And yet, this new Christmas was not only for the wealthy.

Outside the department stores, the Coal Quay bustled with different kinds of wares: live geese squawking in crates, oranges stacked in pyramids, and boiled puddings swaying from hooks. Tinkers from the countryside sold holly and mistletoe. Butchers hawked hams, hawkers sang rhyming jingles, and children weaved through the crowd offering penny carols. Cork's festive life was not segmented strictly by class. The streets, unlike the drawing rooms, were democratic. There, the poor and the comfortable mingled, each participating in the same choreography of gift-giving, song, and spectacle, though from different vantage points.

That night, Tom heard them again, a group of girls from the Presentation Convent, singing in harmonies outside the shop. Their voices cut through the noise like candlelight through fog: *The Wexford Carol, Silent O Moyle, Good Christian Men Rejoice*. Shoppers paused. A few coins clinked in tin cups. An old woman blessed herself. The music, half-rehearsed, half-sacred, connected people more deeply than any display. Even Tom, exhausted, sore-footed, unnoticed, felt lifted by the sound.

Back at Cash & Co., the window display told another kind of story. A young assistant had arranged it himself that morning: a miniature hearth, a doll's cradle, a sprig of holly set carefully on a lace doily. Above, a sign read: 'No Christmas Without Home.' It was a clever bit of advertising, but it struck a chord. For many passers-by, the window scenes mirrored memories: a brother abroad in America, a mother passed the year before, a child now working in Dublin. The emigrants' absences, so deeply felt across Ireland, haunted these displays as much as the poems and prayers.

Retail Christmas in Cork, then, was not only about aspiration, it was about nostalgia. The shop windows offered not only goods but emotions: the illusion of unity, warmth, reunion. Those emotions, commodified, yes, but no less powerful, drew people again and again to stand in the cold and gaze at things they could not afford, and memories they could barely name.

Historians have traced the rise of consumer Christmas in the Victorian British world, a development echoed in Ireland, but with local inflections. In Cork, British commercial traditions mingled with Catholic sensibilities, Gaelic memory, and famine-shaped humility. The candle still burned in the window, but now it flickered beside imported glass and London tins of treacle. The working poor, too, adapted to this new festive economy. They participated as carollers, porters, raffle hosts, sellers of second-hand trinkets. The city's poor may not have shopped in Cash & Co., but they shaped the Christmas atmosphere more than any store clerk.

That night, after the lamps dimmed and the final parcels were wrapped, Tom walked home to Barrack Street with his wage tucked into his coat. He bought two things: a fig for his mother and a red candle, a real beeswax one, not the stubs they usually used. When he arrived, the room was dark and cold. His sister was asleep. His mother was waiting by the hearth. He said nothing, only lit the candle and placed it in the window. She smiled. It was Christmas.

The transformation of Cork's Christmas into a hybrid of faith, commerce, and emotion would shape the decades to come. The department store would rise as the new parish of aspiration. The shop clerk and the carol-singer would become central characters in a city redefining itself through spectacle, trade, and memory. And yet, beyond the department stores and midnight choirs, beyond the candlelit cottages and marbled chapels, something larger pulses beneath the season.

What Is an Irish Christmas?

We close our Prologue with a meditation, not on the true meaning of Christmas, but on how it has endured and evolved in Ireland, and how even now, a single candle in a Cork window speaks across centuries:

> A candle in the window.
> A child asleep in a box bed.
> A hymn in Irish.
> A gift sent from Boston.
> A goose raffled on Barrack Street.
> A letter opened with tears.
> In Ireland, Christmas has never been just a holiday.
> It is an archive.
> A ritual.

To ask, 'What is an Irish Christmas?' is not to seek one answer, but to open a thousand doors. For the Irish do not wear their celebrations on the surface. They bury them in memory; they carry them in ritual, they distil them into symbols, a crib of stones, a chair kept empty at the table. They do not only celebrate Christmas. They inhabit it, quietly, communally, enduringly.

Christmas in Ireland is not a frozen postcard scene of carollers in snow. It is a candle flickering against the Atlantic wind. It is a Mass said with shoes worn paper-thin. It is a feast made of scarcity, a song sung for the absent, a bowl of cream placed reverently beside a fire. It is, above all, a moment of connection, between past and present, the living and the dead, the homeland and the far away. And it is this complex, layered emotional geography, that defines the Irish Christmas more than any imported image or inherited liturgy.

Anthropologists and cultural historians have written about the emotional weight of Irish communal memory. Christmas serves as one of its most resonant rituals. It is a turn in the year, where longing and loss are not banished but invited in, dressed in ritual, made visible by light. This emotional openness is structured not in grand gestures, but in small repetitions. Each act holds a world. Each gesture encodes not only grief but hope, a hope that connection, though frayed by famine, exile, or death, might still hold.

Perhaps no symbol captures the Irish Christmas so powerfully as the empty chair, left at the hearth, at the table, or simply in memory. Technically, it was for the stranger, a spiritual echo of Mary and Joseph's seeking rest. But in practice, it often represented someone gone. That chair

Figure 3. Cork in 1750, Charles Smith, The antient and present state of the county and city of Cork, vol. 1 (Dublin: Reilly, 1750).

became a kind of domestic altar. Some families placed a candle beside it. Others left a slice of pudding, or a note. In the words of one oral history from North Cork: 'We'd leave Da's pipe beside the candle, and Mam would set his spoon as if he might come in yet, through wind or rain.'

Christmas in Ireland occurs in the darkest days of the year. Long nights, low skies, cold winds from the west. And so, it is no accident that light plays such a central role. Not the blaze of chandeliers or electric bulbs, but the steady flame of the household candle.

Lit at dusk on Christmas Eve, the candle in the window is a gesture older than empire, deeper than doctrine. It welcomes the Christ child, but also the neighbour, the traveller, the absent one. It is a flare of hospitality in a country too long known for exile. It says, *We remember you. We wait for you.* That candle, whether in a farmhouse in West Cork, a tenement in Blackpool, or a mansion on Wellington Road, binds all who see it into a shared emotional contract: to endure, to honour, to believe. The Victorian Christmas, exported from London via Dickens, advertising, and empire, introduced holly, plum pudding, gift-giving, and the illusion of familial harmony. Ireland absorbed some of these symbols, particularly among the urban and Anglo-Irish elite. But the Irish Christmas never became wholly Victorian. It remained quieter, humbler, and therefore, perhaps, truer. It honoured not only abundance, but absence. Not only feast, but fast. And it kept, at its core, the flickering thread of hope - *solas 's sonas*, light and happiness - lit against the cold of the world.

Even now, in a world of supermarket hams and LED fairy lights, the DNA of the Irish Christmas holds firm. We still light candles in windows, even if now they are electric. We still leave chairs unfilled. We still read letters from abroad. And when the bells of County Cork's churches ring out on Christmas Eve, they echo not only across the landscape, but across time, calling us back to a thousand homes, a thousand gestures, a thousand lights placed quietly in darkness.

1

Darkness and Light

In the heart of Irish folklore, the themes of darkness and light intertwine in stories that speak to more than physical conditions of night and day. They reflect a deeper human experience, one shaped by resilience in the face of hardship, generosity amidst scarcity and a search for meaning in the shifting seasons of life. Nowhere are these opposites more poignantly expressed than in the folk customs and oral traditions surrounding Christmas. The season of light, marked by candles glowing in cottage windows, was also a time when storms raged, ships were lost at sea, and memories of grief or persecution returned with haunting clarity. These narratives, passed down through generations, do more than recount past events, they illuminate the human capacity to find hope and ritual in even the bleakest circumstances.

The Christmas Candle stands as a profound metaphor within this collection. In every home, as Christmas night descended, the bean-a-tí - the woman of the house - would prepare a single, substantial candle. Whether seated in a meal-filled crock or nestled in a scooped-out turnip, the candle was set not merely for practical light, but as a symbolic beacon for the Holy Family, should they pass through the darkness of night in search of shelter. In the rural villages of West Cork and beyond, this tradition turned modest homes into luminous sanctuaries, each window reflecting not just light, but care, belief, and remembrance.

Yet this illumination often shone against a backdrop of literal and metaphorical darkness. Tales of shipwrecks, like that of The Rio at Oileán Aolbhach or the Iberia off Mizen Head, remind us of the unpredictable ferocity of winter seas. When these tragedies occurred on or around Christmas Day, they transformed what should have been a time of peace into a period of mourning. Families waited for sailors who never came home. Fires burned not just in hearths, but in the remains of broken vessels. And still, candles were lit, because even in mourning, light persisted.

The natural world plays an elemental role in these stories. Storms, fog, and mist are not just weather events but characters themselves, agents of change and sometimes destruction. *An Doine*ann, for instance, recounts a storm so severe that it overturned boats and took lives, yet the tale is told not only as a tragedy but as a witness to endurance. Such storms come and go, but the rituals, like the lighting of candles, remain. This resilience in the face of adversity is perhaps the strongest thread connecting light to darkness in Irish Christmas folklore.

Beyond the physical darkness of winter nights and sea storms, many of the stories delve into more existential shadows. We hear the lament of Timothy Cadogan, condemned and awaiting execution during the festive season. His Christmas is spent in a jail cell rather than a family home. His story, a mix of injustice, sorrow, and ultimate surrender to fate, adds a sobering contrast to the celebratory tone often associated with the season. His plea to God for mercy mirrors the prayers said beside candles in homes across Ireland, though his were said in despair, others were whispered in hope.

Even the light itself, as described in the customs of placing candles in windows or watching for the flicker in an abandoned church on Christmas night, carries a spectral quality. Light in these stories is never simply brightness; it is memory, mystery, and sometimes even a signal from beyond. The people of Kilvilogue, who gather to watch for the ethereal glow in the ruins of an old church, do so not out of superstition, but from a sense of connection to those who came before. In their eyes, the light is a bridge between the past and the present, between those lost and those who remember.

As much as these stories reflect hardship and sorrow, they also honour joy, generosity, and ritual. The act of preparing the Christmas table, not just for guests but for the Holy Family, speaks to the heart of Irish hospitality and reverence. Even when poverty was widespread and food was scarce, families would still set aside bread, butter, and cake, just in case divine visitors arrived. That hope, that instinct to provide despite having little, is itself a form of light.

Thus, the folklore of Christmas in Ireland becomes a meditation on duality. The festive lights shine brighter because they are surrounded by winter's long nights. Stories of shipwreck and loss sit alongside verses of celebration and song. It is in the interplay between darkness and light that the full texture of these tales emerges. They are not romanticised visions of the past but rich, layered narratives that reflect the full human condition.

The Christmas candle, then, reminds us that even in times of uncertainty or suffering, the human spirit seeks to illuminate, to bring warmth where there is cold, companionship where there is loneliness, and meaning where there may be none. This is the essence of folklore: to bind communities together through shared rituals, to make sense of the inexplicable, and to carry light forward into whatever darkness lies ahead.

The stories that follow are taken from the Schools' Collection (1937–1939) a most remarkable folklore archive, created when thousands of schoolchildren across Ireland gathered stories from parents, grandparents, and neighbours. These handwritten notebooks capture local traditions, beliefs, customs, and memories at a moment when many were fading from daily life. Compiled under the direction of the Irish Folklore Commission, the collection preserves the lived voices of rural Ireland, its humour, hardship, and deep sense of community. For County Cork, it provides an irreplaceable record of Christmas customs, weather lore, songs, and stories told beside long vanished hearths.

The Golden Candle

Once upon a time there was a poor man who lived in a small cottage in the woods. He had a wife and three children, and they were very poor. They had no money to buy a Christmas tree or any decorations, and they were very sad.

One day, the man went to the forest to gather some wood. As he was walking through the woods, he saw a beautiful tree with bright red berries. He thought to himself, 'This would make a lovely Christmas tree for my family.' So, he cut down the tree and brought it home.

When he got home, he placed the tree in the corner of the room and decorated it with some candles he had found. That night, as they sat around the tree, they heard a knock at the door. The man opened the door and found a poor old woman standing there. She was cold and hungry, and she asked if she could come in and warm herself by the fire.

The man invited her in and gave her some food and a place to sit by the fire. As they sat together, the old woman told them stories of Christmases long ago, and they all listened with wonder.

The next morning, the man woke up to find that the old woman had left, but she had left behind a beautiful golden candle on the table. The man lit the candle, and from that day on, they never wanted for anything. They had enough food to eat, and their home was always warm and bright. And so, the Christmas candle brought them happiness and prosperity, and they lived happily ever after.[1]

---

[1] The Schools' Collection, Volume 0356, p.259.

The Housewife's Vigil

When night falls on Christmas night the bean-a-tí [housewife] in each house in the country prepares the Christmas candle - usually a pound Candle.

If she has not a candlestick sufficiently large enough to hold the candle, she gets a jam crock and fills it with meal, makes a hole in the centre and puts the candle into it. She makes it firm by pressing the meal around it. Then she covers the crock with coloured papers and decorates it with holly in which are red berries.

If she has not a suitable jam crock, she gets a turnip and scoops out the centre of it just sufficiently large enough to hold the candle. She then fits in the candle and decorates the turnip as she would have decorated the crock.

This candle is let lighting on the window during the while night to show the Holy Family the way should they happen to be passing by. In the country the doors are left on the latch - not locked - lest the Holy Family may need shelter during the night and many housewives let the table in readiness - vessels, bread, butter, sweet cake etc - lest the Holy Family may need something to eat.[2]

---

[2] The Schools' Collection, Volume 0356, p.259.

The Windows of Carbery

It is a great custom among the people of West Cork, or Carbery, to have a lighted Christmas candle in every window of the house on the nights of Christmas Eve, Christmas Day, New Years Eve and Epiphany which is called 'Little Christmas; or the 'Women's Christmas'.

The Women's Christmas is so called in West Cork because the men try to make everything as pleasant as possible for the women so that they can enjoy a peaceful and happy time, the women having worked so hard to make the real Christmas day a happy one for everyone else.

The reason why the candles are lighted is because the little child Jesus is supposed to be passing by and the lights are to guide Him on His way. It is the custom in every house that the youngest child is supposed to light the candles and the oldest person to put them out in the morning. They are left burning all night. These candles are not like the ordinary ones. They are long and thick and each one weighs a pound.

Candle sticks for these candles are made from turnips. At first a good-sized turnip is procured and both ends are cut off so as to make it stand steadily. Then a hold the width of the candle is scooped out of the centre in which the candle is put standing. This improvised candlestick is then beautifully decorated with coloured paper, holly, and berries and is put in the window. On any of these special occasions it is a beautiful sight when going round the country to see every window lighted up.[3]

Collector: Betty Connell, Ardura Beg.

---

[3] The Schools' Collection, Volume 0294, pp.259-261.

An Old Graveyard in Kilvilogue

There is an old Graveyard in Kilvilogue in the Parish of Kilmeen, two miles from Rossmore. There is a ruin of an old Church near the Graveyard. This burial place is closed now. The graves and headstones are still there. On every Christmas Night a light is seen in the ruin of the old Church. The people in this place watch for the light on Christmas Night.[4]

Informant: Annie O' Leary, Knockaneady.

A Shipwreck on the Ilen

About a dozen years ago a small ship loaded with about 150 ton of coal for Old Court arrived in the river near Innisbeg Island about a mile from our school. It arrived late on Christmas eve. It was dark where the crew had her anchored. They then came ashore to Old Court for provisions or messages leaving no one on watch. After two hours when the men returned the ship and cargo of coal were on fire. The part of the ship over water was burned also the top part of the cargo. Some man bought what remained of the wreck for a small price and tried to bring ashore some coal out of it. A part of the wrecked schooner can still be seen in the River Ilen near Innisbeg.[5]

Collector: Lizzie Minihane, Creagh.
Informant: Mr. Minihane.

---

[4] The Schools' Collection, Volume 0310, Page 056
[5] The Schools' Collection, Volume 0297, p.87.

The Sinking of The Rio at Oileán Aolbhach

On Christmas Day 1888 a schooner was sailing up towards the Dursey head going to America. She was called "The Rio". She was a very old boat, and the captain and crew were afraid to chance the voyage across. Instead of keeping going west, they turned down along the south-west of Dursey Island. They sounded the ground first under Cill Mhichíl but they thought it too shallow. They turned her right around again and put up full sail and steered straight for Oileán Aolbhach. The Dursey people were watching him. She struck about mid-way on the little island, and she staggered back with the blow, but she didn't sink. He moved out a little and struck her the second time. This did the business. She began to sink, and the crew lowered a little boat they had, and four of them went into her. The Dursey people were out to mass and when they were coming home, they saw the Rio, and they set out for Oileán Aolbhach to take off the men. The mate was up on the stern of the schooner still and when the boat came, he threw himself into the sea and swam towards her although there was a grand swell there at the time. They landed them east in Leac and they stayed in a house in Baile 'nChalaidh that night. There was nothing in the old schooner but three or four bags of flour, and they were as black as the soot. She sank about an hour after striking. The mast could be seen from Dursey during big tides, but a year or so afterwards, she was smashed up by the storms and that was the last heard of "The Rio".[6]

Collector: Seán Ó H-Urdaill, Cill Mhichíl.

---

[6] The Schools' Collection, Volume 0274, pp.98-100.

West Cork Christmas Shipwrecks

There were shipwrecks up to the year 1910 off the Mizen Head, Co. Cork, until the British Government erected a signal station there. The Iberia was wrecked off the Mizen Head one Christmas Eve in 1909. This was the last ship to be lost off the south-west coast of Ireland. This ship was laden with guncotton. This wreck was highly dangerous to other ships on the same line because when guncotton becomes water-soaked it is liable to burst and damage the ship which comes in contact with it. The stewardesses and the chief officers were the only lives lost. A dense mist enveloped the rugged headland, and the poor ship went to her doom. Attempts at rescue were impossible as it is far away from civilisation.

The other ship which was wrecked off this coast was the Memphis, laden with a general cargo bound from Canada. She went to her doom off Bird Island off Kilcrohane, Co. Cork in a bad storm. There was no loss of lives in this disaster as the cattle on board were alive, and the crew jumped on their backs to carry them to safety. This disaster occurred in a bad storm while on her homeward journey. She ran on the treacherous rocks off Dunmanus. Several people looted her, but the law interfered and prevented them.[7]

Collector: Fred Evans, Clashadoo.
Informant: Mrs Evans.

---

[7] The Schools' Collection, Volume 0285, pp.170-171.

An Doineann

Storms rage frequently in this locality owing to its bleak position near the Atlantic Ocean. Sometimes a land storm takes place, other times it is a sea storm and very often both take place at the same time.

A fearful storm raged through the neighbourhood about nine years ago. This storm prevailed during the festival of Christmas, and it was not a very happy one for the people as they were in dread of the gale. Many houses were broken, and a few were left almost roofless. Hay-sheds were knocked and over-turned. Many tombstones were knocked in the local cemeteries, and a number of other damages were also caused.

A crew of fishermen went out fishing in a seine boat in a place called Tráigh An Phéarla about two miles from this district. The fishermen left the coast early in the evening. They were not gone very far when signs of a storm appeared. They kept rowing however and after a little while the storm arose. They tried to bring the boat back to the strand, but they did not succeed in doing so. The boat was overturned, and every member of the crew was thrown into the sea and drowned. The boat was completely destroyed, and the tragedy was considered to be one of the most disastrous ever witnessed in the locality.[8]

Collector: Máire Ní Úrdail, Cloan.
Informant: Seán Ó Ceallaigh, aged 68, Tailor.

---

[8] The Schools' Collection, Volume 0274, pp.462-463.

The Christmas Shipwreck in Whiddy

The night was wet and dreary
And the wind from the south west was blowing
And he never knew of danger,
Until he was seated upon a heap of stones.

If the captain may haul home his traces,
And steer eastward a little more
He would avoid all danger
And come safe on the sandbank shore.

American beef and bacon
And tea from East India shore,
And you'd hear the women stating,
And lamenting their Christmas store.

One night about fifty years ago, a boat laden with provisions for Christmas left Bantry for Whiddy. A thick fog came in and after several hour's rowing the boat grounded on a rock close to the Quay. The passengers escaped but all in the boat was destroyed.[9]

Collector: Maighréad Ní Laoghaire, Reenaknock, Co. Cork
Informant: Donnachadh Ua Laoghaire

---

[9] The Schools' Collection, Volume 0284, pp.240-241.

The Trial of Timothy Cadogan

The following song was composed about Timothy Cadogan, Coomdelame who was hanged for the murder of William Birde, a Bantry landlord.

Farewell to friends and relatives at home and far away,
The sword of death will cut away my thread of life this day,
With heart and hand I write those lines for my country men to see,
That I am going to face my God on a shameful gallow tree.

A sad and dreary month has passed since I was guilty found,
For the murder of W. S. Birde that day in Bantry town,
On the eleventh day of January I am summoned to appear,
Before the judgement seat of God my sentence there to hear.

It was cruel and wicked evidence that swore my life away,
I never thought it would be my lot to die in Cork County jail,
Till December 1900 my prosecutors swore,
I am the man who shot Willie Bird and left him in his gore

When cruel and wicked evidence against me did appear
The jury did not hesitate to brand me with the crime
The judge in passing sentence to me made this reply
On the eleventh day of January Tim Cadogan you shall die

From the courthouse dock I was sent back to a shameful gallows tree,
Where I must end my youthful days in pain and agony
May God forgive my enemies who brought me here to die,
Their conscience will accuse them as long as they are alive.

In health I was at home for many a Christmas night.
But here inside Cork County jail Ill spend the last in life.
May God forgive my enemies and those I love so dear.
When I am in my prison grave for me they will shed a tear.

My hour it is approaching for death I must prepare
Before the throne of justice my soul will soon appear
When the Virgin queen of martyrs will be my advocate,
For God to show me mercy on the great accounting day.[10]

---

[10] The Schools' Collection, Volume 0288, pp.314-316.

A CONDEMNED MAN'S WICKED HOPE.

At Cork Assizes, yesterday, Timothy Cadogan was convicted of the murder of William Bird, land agent, at Bantry, on the 26th of February last. Prisoner, who had been tried at the summer assizes when the jury disagreed, was sentenced to be hanged on the 11th of January. After sentence of death had been passed upon the prisoner he became very violent, and expressed the hope that before 12 months someone would avenge his death on Dr. Bird, the murdered man's brother, who was a witness in the case.

AN IRISH MURDER TRIAL.

DISAGREEMENT OF THE JURY.

At Cork Assizes yesterday a county common jury, who had been three days investigating a charge of murder against Timothy Cadogan, disagreed, and were discharged. According to the evidence for the prosecution, William Bird, land agent, Bantry, was shot three times whilst in his office collecting rents. A shop assistant named Dennis, engaged underneath the office, heard the firearms discharged, and swore that he saw the prisoner descending the staircase, placing a revolver in his pocket. Cadogan is an evicted tenant.

Figure 4. Nottingham Evening Post, 21 July 1900, p.2.
Figure 5. Manchester Courier, 12 December 1900, p.7.

CORONER AND EXECUTIONER.

Timothy Cadogan was executed at Cork on Fr[iday], for the murder of Mr. Williams Bird, la[nd] agent, Bantry, last February. Cadogan, who was a[n] evicted tenant, shot Mr. Bird dead while the latt[er] was receiving the rents in his office. The ju[ry] disagreed at the summer assizes, but the man w[as] convicted in December. After being sentence[d] Cadogan, pointing to Dr. Bird, the murdered gentl[e]man's brother, shouted, "I hope I'll be avenged befo[re] I am twelve months gone." Cadogan showed gre[at] resignation until the small hours of on Friday mornin[g] when, after a restless night, he endeavoured to c[ut] his throat with the iron tip of his boot. The warde[r] in charge, however, interposed and prevented hi[m] from inflicting any serious injury. The chapla[in] arrived at six o'clock, and spent the time with t[he] condemned man, who calmed down completely a[nd] met his fate courageously, walking to the scaffo[ld] without assistance, and giving the responses to t[he] service for the dead, which the chaplain recited. [At] six o'clock he heard mass and received the Sacr[a]ment, after which he partook of a good breakfa[st]. The inquest was opened at ten o'clock, when Coron[er] Horgan asked if Billington, the executioner, w[as] present, but the governor of the gaol said he had le[ft] the prison, whereupon a noisy scene ensued betwe[en] the Coroner and the gaol officials. Ultimately t[he] Coroner adjourned the inquiry for ten days, a[nd] intimated that if Billington did not then attend would dismiss the jury.—The Coroner has issued warrant for the arrest of Billington, because, it stated, the executioner refused to obey his summo[ns] t[o] attend and give evidence at the inquest. T[he] warrant is in the hands of the police.

Billington, the executioner, who keeps a public-hou[se] in Bolton, returned home on Saturday, having be[en] escorted by Irish police to Holyhead. In connect[ion] with the issue by the Cork Coroner of a warrant for [his] arrest because of his refusal to attend the inquest [on] the man hanged there on the previous day. Billingt[on] asserts that it is not customary for him to attend su[ch] inquiries, and he refuses to do so in this case unle[ss]

Figure 6. Runcorn Guardian, 16 January 1901, p.8.

Reflections

As this chapter draws to a close, we are left with a mosaic of tales, some humble, others haunting, all united by the shared human experience of navigating the liminal space between darkness and light. The stories gathered here are not just recollections of past events but living embodiments of cultural memory. Through candles lit against the long December night, through storms weathered and lives remembered, we see how folklore holds a mirror to the most profound of life's dualities.

Christmas, with all its warmth, radiance, and ritual, does not banish darkness, it dwells within it. The act of lighting a candle on Christmas Eve is not done in the brightness of day but as dusk sets in, as the world outside becomes still, as shadows stretch long across the land. This contrast is what gives the act its power. The candle's flame stands resilient not in opposition to darkness, but within it. It is this coexistence that defines Irish folklore. Light does not conquer darkness, it lives alongside it, flickering gently, reminding us that hope can persist even in sorrow, that joy can exist beside grief.

The folkloric accounts of shipwrecks, often falling around Christmas, highlight this interplay with vivid poignancy. The stories of The Rio and The Iberia, of boats dashed against the rocks and crews scrambling for survival, evoke both physical darkness, the treacherous, fog-bound seas, and emotional devastation, as lives are lost at what should be a time of gathering and celebration. Yet, even here, light makes an appearance. Whether it is the lantern of a rescuer, the candle still glowing in a coastal window, or the prayers offered in memory of those lost, there is always some glimmer that refuses to go out.

The motif of the Christmas candle itself is more than just a domestic custom, it is an act of storytelling. Each family that lit a candle was participating in a ritual that connected them not just to the Holy Family, but to generations of their own community. The youngest child lighting the candle and the oldest putting it out reflects a continuum, a passage of time, of memory, of belief. It is a simple act with profound meaning, symbolising renewal, lineage, and the ever-present potential for grace.

In a world often marked by hardship, such rituals served to humanise suffering and frame it within a structure of meaning. The storm described in "An Doineann" was devastating, yet the story survives not as a list of losses, but as testimony to resilience. It becomes a way for a community to honour what was endured, to ensure that the names and the pain are not forgotten. In this way, light is not merely about illumination but about recognition. We light candles to see, yes, but also to be seen, to ensure that the departed, the poor, the persecuted, and the ordinary are not lost to history's oblivion.

Other stories, like that of the graveyard light at Kilvilogue, blur the boundaries between the living and the dead. The glowing apparition on Christmas night invites us to consider how light can also be a signal, a guide from one realm to another. Whether as ghost, spirit, or miracle, the light affirms presence. It tells us that absence is never total, that something of those who came before remains. This spiritual element in Irish Christmas folklore taps into a broader cultural understanding of time as cyclical, not linear. Just as the seasons turn from winter to spring, just as the longest night gives way to longer days, so too does memory rise again in ritual.

There is also humour, humility, and humanity in these tales. From the improvisation of turnip candlesticks to the deeply human prayers offered for a child lost at sea or a man facing the gallows, the stories never drift into abstraction. They are grounded in lived experience, in the clutter of a country kitchen, in the frost on a fishing boat, in the quiet hush of midnight Mass. The stories are not perfect, nor are the people within them. But that is precisely their strength. In folklore, it is not perfection we seek, but truth, the truth of how people lived, what they feared, how they loved, and where they found meaning.

In the case of Timothy Cadogan, the darkness is not metaphorical. It is the gloom of a prison cell, the shadow of injustice, the finality of death. And yet, even here, there is a strange light: the clarity of conscience, the plea for mercy, the sorrow of separation. His verses are not just self-defence, they are a final act of expression, an attempt to claim humanity in the face of annihilation. That, too, is a form of light.

Likewise, the stories about landlords, about local ghosts, about the Holy Family wandering the night roads of West Cork, these are stories that carry deep moral weight. They remind us of hospitality, of justice, of the need to care for those we may never see. The candles in the windows were not just decorations. They were promises. "You are not alone," they said. "You are welcome here."

In today's world, where electric lights flood every city and artificial brightness erases the stars, these tales ask us to consider what it means to truly appreciate the darkness. Not to fear it, but to honour it as the stage upon which light performs its most important role. The Irish rural Christmas was once full of such darkness, literal and metaphorical, but it was never empty. It held song and story, prayer and presence, memory and mystery.

Folklore is not static. These traditions evolve, but the spirit behind them remains. The candle may now be an electric bulb. The Christmas table may groan with store-bought abundance rather than sparse offerings of bread and cake. But the impulse to mark the moment, to create light in darkness, lives on.

In a time when many people experience metaphorical winters of isolation, grief, or uncertainty, the lessons of these stories grow more relevant, not less. They teach us to cherish even the smallest light, to tend it with care, to offer it freely. They show us that in every act of remembrance, hospitality, resistance, or love, we rekindle something ancient and enduring.

So let us close this chapter with a candle lit in the window of memory. Let it burn not just for the Holy Family, but for all the wandering souls who seek warmth in cold seasons. For the sailors and shepherds, the mothers and martyrs, the children and the old who have kept these stories alive. May the light of their words guide us, as it guided generations before, through the darkness, and into the heart of Christmas.

2

When the Sea Came for Christmas

The sea has always shaped the imagination and destiny of Ireland, and few places reflect this more starkly than the southern coastline of County Cork. From the Old Head of Kinsale to Ballycotton Bay, the Atlantic presses in with restless persistence. This liminal space between hope and tragedy has, as we have seen, witnessed countless stories of daring, desperation, and demise. Among them, the maritime disasters occurring during the Christmas season possess a particular poignancy. They remind us that, even in the season of light and joy, darkness and sorrow are never far from the shore.

In this chapter, we delve into the phenomenon of winter shipwrecks, specifically those that occurred during December and early January over several centuries. The archive is rich and sobering. These were no isolated incidents: the frequency with which vessels were lost, often within sight of land, reveals a perilous maritime history that shaped not only the physical coastline but the emotional and cultural landscape of its people.

The clustering of these tragedies around the Christmas season adds an emotional gravity to the narrative. For the seafaring communities of Cork, the yuletide was not only a time of celebration but one of anxiety. The arrival of winter gales, thick fogs, and unpredictable tides made coastal navigation particularly hazardous. Mariners pushed hard to make port in time for Christmas; merchants hoped to unload goods for the festive markets; emigrants longed to arrive home for the holidays. But often, the sea had other plans.

This is not simply a catalogue of loss; Woven into these tales are deeper threads of folklore, communal memory, and social change. Many of the wrecks recounted here are remembered not only through official records but through oral tradition, ballads, and local folklore. In some cases, wreckage remained visible for decades, becoming part of the local landscape like ghostly footprints of lives lost. In others, the events prompted legal action, community efforts at salvage, and, in rare cases, prosecutions for looting or even deliberate wrecking.

The Christmas timing of these wrecks also envokes powerful symbolic associations: the tension between light and darkness, life and death, welcome and exile. In Irish tradition, Christmas Eve and Christmas

Day were charged with mystical significance. It was said that animals could speak, that graves opened slightly to allow the dead to hear Mass, that candles lit in windows would guide the Holy Family. Against such a backdrop, a sudden catastrophe at sea felt both sacred and tragic, imbued with the emotional resonance of a season meant to be joyful.

These shipwrecks, then, do not just represent lost cargoes and sunken hulls. They are stories of interrupted journeys, of communities shaken by loss, and of nature's indifference to human desire. They remind us of the fragility of life, even as the world around us celebrates birth and renewal.

Over the course of this chapter, we will examine notable shipwrecks that occurred during the Christmas season from the early 18th century to the early 20th. We will consider the economic, meteorological, and navigational conditions that made Cork's coast so treacherous in winter. We will draw on contemporary newspaper reports, court records, and local folklore to explore the human cost of these disasters. And we will ask: What does it mean for tragedy to strike during a season meant to embody peace? In doing so, this chapter seeks not only to document a series of events but to explore how the memory of maritime tragedy has become part of the cultural consciousness of coastal Cork, etched into stone, song, and story.

Wrecks in the Age of Sail

The eighteenth century marked a period of growing maritime commerce for Ireland. Cork, in particular, developed into one of the busiest provisioning ports in the British Empire, supplying the Royal Navy and merchant vessels alike. But this prosperity came at a cost. With increased shipping came increased risk, and the winter seas off the Cork coast claimed vessel after vessel, especially during the Christmas period, when gales were frequent, and ports were crowded with ships hoping to make harbour before the turn of the year.

One of the earliest recorded Christmas wrecks in the area occurred in 1724, when three unnamed vessels were lost at the Cove of Cork on Christmas Day. Only one man from one of the ships survived. This event, reported a month later in January 1725, was a harbinger of the century to come, one marked by repeated tragedy, as ships were often wrecked within sight of the port they sought.

Figure 7. Kinsale in 1750, Charles Smith, The antient and present state of the county and city of Cork, vol. 1 (Dublin: Reilly, 1750).

These early losses were sparsely recorded, but their human cost was no less real, remembered in parish records and the oral traditions of the surrounding villages.

In December 1739, the coast around Youghal witnessed another triple tragedy. The Squire, arriving from Virginia with a cargo of tobacco and staves, was lost alongside the John of Barnstable, laden with coal. A third, unnamed ship, carrying tallow and hides bound for Rotterdam, also succumbed to the tempest. These were not mere isolated incidents; rather, they formed part of a wider pattern in which vessels arriving from the Atlantic met their end in the narrowing channels and shoals of the southern Irish coast. Many were caught unawares by sudden changes in weather, or else undone by poor charts and unreliable pilotage.

Not all disaster came from storm alone. In December 1740, the Unity, a sloop from Southampton, ran aground east of Cork Harbour. The wreck was quickly descended upon by locals, who stripped it of cargo and timbers. The act of plundering wrecked ships, while condemned by the authorities, was often seen by impoverished coastal communities as a tragic windfall, an ambivalent gift from the sea. In this case, however, justice was unusually swift. A man named John Fleming was convicted for his role in dismantling the wreck and was sentenced to hang. His punishment reveals the tightening grip of legal authority over the folk customs of salvage, which had long operated in the grey space between necessity and criminality.

Later in the decade, the coast near Roberts Cove saw a series of losses. In December 1750, the ship Twins, bound from Nantes, was lost here. Eight years later, in 1758, two more ships, the Pembroke and the Oswego, both from Bristol and bound for New York, were wrecked off the Cork coast, with twelve men drowned from the Pembroke. These vessels carried more than just cargo: they were part of the transatlantic trade network connecting Ireland, Britain, Europe, and the American colonies. The loss of such ships at Christmas was doubly felt, financially, as trade was disrupted, and emotionally, as the prospect of festive reunion was shattered.

Another remarkable wreck from the late 1750s involved a London-to-Yarmouth ship carrying wine and brandy. In December 1759, she foundered in Ballycotton Bay, one of the region's most perilous stretches of coast.

The cargo, steeped in festivity and luxury, only deepens the irony of its demise during the most celebratory time of the year.

Reports mention that the captain and four crew members were saved, but the cargo, presumably a holiday bounty for British markets, was lost to the sea.

The year 1763 brought further disaster. On December 26, a collier captained by a man named Vernon was wrecked off Ballycotton. In the same storm, nine boats anchored near the cove were also lost, with lives reported missing. This clustering of maritime incidents underscores the treacherous volatility of Cork's coast in December. The coal trade was particularly exposed; ships were often overloaded, and their crews desperate to deliver cargo before Christmas, a critical time for heating fuel in both cities and towns.

In 1764, the Union, bound from Bristol to Limerick and Galway, was lost at Cork, and the following year, the Britannia met a similar fate in Ballycotton Bay, while en route from Dublin and Liverpool to Colchester. Contemporary accounts noted that "everything was destroyed by the country people", again pointing to the tension between local survival instincts and the growing criminalisation of wreck salvage by maritime authorities.

The Philadelphia, lost in December 1772, is a particularly illustrative example. She initially struck the bar while leaving Youghal Harbour, was refloated, and then, fatally, struck a rock on her return. This chain of misfortune, mechanical failure, poor navigation, and bad luck, typifies many wrecks of the period. Nature did not need to act alone; human error often helped seal a ship's fate.

In the closing decades of the century, the pattern continued. The Peggy (1785), the Hope (1787), the Friendship (1788), and the Nancy (1794) were all lost along the coast from Youghal to Kinsale, many within the narrow band of days leading up to Christmas. Several ships were driven ashore by gales. Others were scuttled deliberately, such as the Two Friends, whose master, John Allen of Ringaskiddy, was jailed in 1794 for looting his own vessel before sinking it at the harbour's mouth. Fraud, too, played a role in maritime loss.

A particularly grim year was 1798, when three ships, the Boyd, the Dispatch, and the Charlotte, were wrecked in separate incidents near Kinsale and Cork. While the crews of the Boyd and Dispatch were reportedly saved, the Charlotte met a darker fate: only a boy survived. The repetition of these events year after year left scars not only on families but on entire coastal communities, who lived with the constant threat of sudden death during the festive season.

Figure 8. Youghal in 1750, Charles Smith, The antient and present state of the county and city of Cork, vol. 1 (Dublin: Reilly, 1750).

By the close of the 18th century, maritime Christmas tragedies had become almost expected, spoken of with dread, memorialised in church records and graveyards, and occasionally immortalised in ballads and local lore. As ships grew in size and number, and as trade routes expanded, the risks only increased.

These events underscore the fragility of 18th-century seafaring and the deep emotional resonance of wintertime loss. For communities already living with hardship, a Christmas shipwreck was more than just a maritime incident: it was a rupture of hope at the very moment when hope was meant to be most abundant. It is perhaps no surprise, then, that many of these wrecks entered the realm of folk memory, stories whispered by the hearth or recited in old age, anchoring personal and collective grief to the unpredictable waters of the Cork coast.

Storms of Progress

The nineteenth century was a time of enormous transformation in seafaring. Steam power began to challenge sail, ports grew busier, and transatlantic shipping accelerated dramatically. Cork remained a vital node in British and international maritime routes. Yet despite technological advances, the Cork coast remained unforgiving, and the winter sea showed little mercy. Christmas, traditionally a time of reunion and homecoming, became, for many, a time marked by loss, as ships foundered in sight of safety, dashed against rocks, or sunk beneath gale-driven waves.

On Christmas Day 1803, the wreck of HMS Suffisante a Royal Navy sloop-of-war that went aground off Spike Island during a gale. Despite her experienced crew, the ship broke apart in heavy seas. Seven sailors drowned, and three were killed by a falling mast, stark evidence that even naval vessels were no match for winter storms. The scene, a warship splintering on the coast at the height of Christmas, must have left a deep impression on those stationed nearby.

That same decade saw repeated loss. In December 1800, two ships were lost: the Bellona, carrying coal from Whitehaven, struck rocks near Ballycotton and sank (though the crew were saved); and the Gravalia, sailing from Spain to Hamburg, wrecked near Kinsale. While lives were preserved in both cases, these incidents are reminders of how common winter shipwrecks had become, routine tragedies that rarely reached national news but were etched into the local consciousness.

Figure 9. Entrance to Cork Harbour.

In 1801, the New Thompson sloop struck Youghal bar in dense fog on December 3rd, losing its rudder and drifting ashore. Two of the crew perished, one dashed on rocks while trying to swim to safety, another succumbing to cold during the night. Three survivors were rescued the next day by locals. This pattern - fog, grounding, failed escape, and community rescue - was typical of the period. The shoreline communities often served as impromptu first responders, with fishermen, farmers, and women risking their lives to save others.

By mid-century, even the growing adoption of steam could not prevent disaster. On December 13, 1844, the paddle-steamer Vanguard, en route from Dublin to Cork, struck the Cow and Calf rocks off Roches Point during a stiff south-westerly gale. Fortunately, all passengers and crew were rescued, and the ship was eventually salved. But others weren't so lucky. A week later, on December 20, part of a ship's boat washed into Rocky Bay, and soon after, the mainmast of a schooner, broken off cleanly at the rigging, drifted into Ringabella Bay. These fragments were all that remained of an unnamed vessel, presumed to have foundered off the coast in another silent, unobserved wreck.

The coast's vulnerability was laid bare during the great Christmas storm of December 1825, one of the most destructive maritime weather events of the century. From the 19th to the 20th of December, a fierce south-easterly gale battered the Cork coastline, causing ship after ship to run aground, be driven ashore, or founder at sea. At Ballyandreen Bay, the Britannia of Padstow struck a rock and was dashed to pieces, only the captain survived. On the same days, eight other ships, including the Glasgow, Laura, Union, Jane, Ceres, Repute, Expedition, and the Portuguese schooner Diligente, were reported wrecked or severely damaged in or near the Cove of Cork.

This storm highlighted several dangers. First, the overcrowding of anchorages: many ships sought refuge in Cork Harbour simultaneously, increasing the risk of collisions and fouled anchors. Second, the inadequacy of warning systems: even with barometers and storm signals, sailors had little time to react to sudden squalls. Third, the persistence of local salvage, some cargoes were looted as ships broke apart near shore. These events weren't just maritime misfortunes; they were public dramas, with crowds lining the shore to watch, mourn, or assist.

Later in the century, similar patterns continued. The Eliza, wrecked on Christmas Day 1816, filled with water while attempting to go from Cove to Cork. In 1814, no fewer than five ships, including the Apollo, Lisbon Packet, and Maria, were either wrecked or severely damaged near Cork, Rocky Bay, and Cuskinny. The Maria was lost with all hands, a tragedy during a Christmas season already marked by national hardship. Ireland was descending into pre-Famine instability, and each such loss was a blow to local morale and economy.

The stories that entered folklore often involved not just physical destruction but eerie or extraordinary details. The wreck of the Helenslea in 1881, though the collision itself occurred in September, became deeply associated with Christmas as the bodies of the lost sailors were buried on December 25. Nine men perished when the Cunard liner Catalonia struck the barque in Cork Harbour. Some survivors were rescued, but the rapid sinking, within three minutes, remains one of the deadliest maritime incidents in the harbour's history.

Another grim example was the Princess Royal, wrecked on Christmas Eve 1878 below Camden Fort. Gale conditions prevented the Roches Point coastguard and Queenstown Lifeboat from reaching the wreck. Not a single crew member survived. To die within sight of lights on land, on the threshold of Christmas, gives this tragedy a stark poignancy.

Throughout the century, Cork's coasts swallowed schooners, brigs, barques, and steamers alike. While the record is full of names, the Hope, the Nancy, the Celandine, the Diana, many vessels went unnamed in reports, their crews unrecorded, their stories unspoken. But the cost was real: each shipwreck was a sundering of lives and families, often on the eve of reunion. These tragedies left a mark not only on the coastal rocks, but on the cultural memory of the region.

Church services were held for lost mariners. Christmas vigils sometimes doubled as mourning. In graveyards from Youghal to Kinsale, stones bear the names of captains and crew who perished just miles from shore. Meanwhile, local lore, like that surrounding the Phantom Ship of Ballycotton or the Wreckers of Ringabella, absorbed these wrecks into cautionary tales and supernatural narratives.

In sum, the 19th century brought technological progress, but no reduction in maritime peril. As Cork's shipping lanes grew busier and more vital to imperial and industrial economies, the cost in human life, especially during the cold, volatile weeks around Christmas, remained tragically constant.

Modernity Meets the Deep

As the 20th century dawned, maritime technology stood at a new threshold. Steam engines had become the norm, wireless communication was beginning to link vessels with shore stations, and shipping companies invested in stronger steel hulls, better lifeboats, and organised rescue protocols. Yet, despite these advances, the Cork coast remained treacherous, especially during the short, storm-lashed days of winter. Christmas, still bound in tradition and expectation, offered no reprieve from the sea's enduring indifference.

The wreck of the Sente (or Santo) on Christmas Day 1900 is a sobering opening to this new era. A newly built dredger on her maiden voyage from Glasgow to Formosa, the Sente encountered trouble off Power Head, near Cork Harbour. Heavy weather developed, and the vessel began to list severely. In a matter of hours, she overturned. Despite the proximity to shore and the efforts of a pilot boat, twelve crew members drowned. Only five survived. The Sente's loss was especially poignant; it was not an aged ship weakened by years of service, but a symbol of engineering progress. The sea, however, showed no favouritism.

This theme recurred throughout the century: proximity to safety was no guarantee of rescue. The El Zorro, a tanker struck by a German U-boat on December 28th, 1915, off the Old Head of Kinsale, stands as one of the few examples of wartime shipwrecks along this coast during the Christmas period. One crewman died in the initial attack; another perished during an attempted transfer operation amid gale-force winds. Later that night, the stricken ship, dragging its anchors in the storm, drifted ashore at Man of War Cove and was completely destroyed. This incident not only illustrated the added dangers of war at sea but also the vulnerability of merchant shipping, even within sight of Ireland's coastline.

The two World Wars intensified the risk of sailing near Cork's coast, but even in peacetime, Christmas remained perilous. Ships still wrecked in storms or due to navigational error, and technological advancement was still often rendered impotent in the face of nature's force.

One particularly tragic tale, though the actual wreck occurred earlier in the year, became part of the region's Christmas memory: the Helenslea, a large barque inbound from San Francisco to Queenstown, was struck by the Cunard liner Catalonia in September 1881. The vessel sank within three minutes. Though the majority of survivors were rescued by the Catalonia's crew, nine sailors died, making it one of the deadliest shipping incidents in Cork Harbour. Their burial on Christmas Day bound the tragedy to the festive calendar, intertwining grief with ritual.

Moving through the early 20th century, Cork's growing infrastructure did little to lessen winter's impact on maritime traffic. The sea near Roches Point, Ringabella, and Ballycotton continued to claim vessels, often in fog or violent wind. The Sir Redvers Buller, a War Department steamer, grounded in dense fog on December 6, 1899, at Canavan's Point, a common graveyard for ships. She was refloated the next morning, an exception to the usual fate, but the incident was a reminder that even official or military vessels were not immune to Cork's disorienting weather systems.

The 20th century also bore witness to numerous near-misses, ships that grounded but were later salvaged, such as the Vanguard in 1844 or the Alliance in 1860. Yet these events, even without loss of life, contributed to the cumulative anxiety of seafaring near Cork in winter. The stress of navigating narrow passages like the Sound, avoiding submerged rocks such as Cow and Calf, or anchoring in high seas was unrelenting. For many captains, a winter voyage past Power Head or the Old Head of Kinsale was more ordeal than routine.

By the mid-20th century, air and radio communications allowed faster responses to maritime emergencies. Still, Christmas wrecks continued. Oral tradition, especially in coastal villages such as Ballycotton, Youghal, and Kinsale, kept these stories alive. Some of the worst events from previous centuries became incorporated into local folklore. Lights seen at sea during Christmas Eve were said to be the souls of drowned sailors. In some areas, candles were placed in windows not only for the Holy Family, as tradition dictated, but also to guide lost mariners home.

The combination of historic trauma and maritime dependency shaped Cork's relationship with the sea into something close to reverence and fear. For many coastal families, Christmas was not only a time of religious observance but of waiting, waiting for the return of fishermen, merchantmen, or naval personnel. Wreckage found on beaches was often inspected first not for value but for identification, did it belong to a neighbour? A son? A husband?

Shipwrecks such as that of the El Zorro, the Princess Royal, or the Helenslea resonated beyond the immediate tragedy. They were cautionary tales, reminders that Ireland's identity as an island was more than symbolic, it was precarious. The water that fed, connected, and protected also betrayed.

As the century progressed into the post-war period, larger ships and improved navigation reduced, but did not eliminate, winter disasters.

Yet the psychological toll remained. Coastal towns kept rescue crews on standby during Christmas storms. Stories of men rowing into the surf to save strangers were passed down through generations. Songs were written. Masses were offered. And the sea, each December, waited.

Reflection

The coastline of Cork is a place of contradictions. It is both the gateway and the guard, a source of sustenance and sorrow. During the Christmas season, a time so closely tied to family, faith, and the warmth of home, the wreckage of ships off the Cork coast strikes with a particular poignancy. These maritime disasters do not merely mark historical events; they reverberate through the emotional, cultural, and spiritual memory of a people shaped by the sea.

The long chronicle of Christmas-time shipwrecks, from the three unnamed vessels lost in 1724 to the Sente's capsizing in 1900 and the torpedoing of the El Zorro in 1915, reads not only as a record of maritime disaster, but as a seasonal counterpoint to the joy, hope, and light of the holiday period. Where hearths were lit and candles placed in windows for the Holy Family, there were other lights too: the flares of distress signals, the glow of a vessel burning offshore, the lanterns of search parties combing storm-lashed beaches for survivors, or for bodies.

Each wreck, whether of a named vessel like the Peggy or Unity, or an anonymous craft dashed on the rocks of Ballycotton Bay, threads itself into a wider narrative of transience and vulnerability. For seafaring communities, Christmas was always accompanied by the knowledge that the season's most sacred celebrations could be shattered by news from the sea. The liturgy of the church and the liturgy of the waves operated side by side, one offering comfort, the other demanding reverence.

What emerges most clearly from this litany of loss is the sheer unpredictability of maritime life. Ships well-stocked and well-crewed, with experienced captains and sound cargoes, were undone in a single squall. Entire crews vanished without a trace, leaving behind widows, orphans, and haunting legends. Others narrowly escaped and became part of local lore, living reminders of the knife-edge balance between survival and tragedy. The Rising Sun might be refloated and saved; the Princess Royal's crew would not be so fortunate.

Many of these tragedies took place within sight of land. Villagers at Roches Point, Cove, or Youghal could sometimes witness the desperate final moments of a ship's struggle against wind and tide. The helplessness of onlookers, too late to intervene, too far to reach, too few to make a difference, compounded the sorrow. Such experiences led to the development of lifeboat services and improved coastal rescue infrastructure. But long before formal agencies existed, these communities were already trained by grief to respond with courage.

From a historical standpoint, the clustering of these shipwrecks during December reveals more than just weather patterns. It illuminates the rhythms of trade and migration: ships eager to deliver cargo before year's end, crews hoping to be home for Christmas, naval vessels moving under strict timetables, and emigrants fleeing famine or seeking new lives abroad. Christmas was not just a dangerous time to sail; it was also a time many risked the journey because the stakes, personal and economic, were so high.

In this way, these shipwrecks also underscore the fragility of global connections. The Nancy, lost near Kinsale in 1794, carried coal from Swansea; the Friendship, wrecked in 1788, was bound for the Mediterranean; the El Zorro, torpedoed in 1915, brought oil from foreign ports. These were not isolated voyages; they were nodes in vast economic and political networks. This destruction, often within miles of their destination, illustrates the limitations of even the most ambitious human systems when set against nature's will.

And yet, from devastation came rituals of remembrance and resilience. Candles placed in windows came to symbolise not just religious tradition, but solidarity with those at sea. Prayers were offered not only for the Christ child, but for lost sons, brothers, and fathers. Churches in Cobh, Skibbereen, and Bantry rang their bells in mourning as much as celebration.

The narratives surrounding these wrecks often blend fact with folklore. The burning bush at Ballacummer, the ghostly Mass served by a penitent priest, or the golden candle left by a mysterious stranger all reflect a cultural response to grief that is not strictly historical, but deeply human. In the absence of certainty, communities turned to story to understand and endure. The wrecks became more than tragedies, they became metaphors for fate, faith, and the thin veil between the known and the unknown.

In a way, these tales and truths merge into a form of cultural memory that transcends mere documentation. The wreck of the Charlotte, where all perished but a single boy, is remembered not only for its facts, but for what it signifies: innocence adrift in the wake of catastrophe. The Catalonia's collision with the Helenslea is not only a maritime accident, it is a story of rescue amid ruin, of failure and redemption side by side.

The sea off the Cork coast has always been a frontier, not just between land and water, but between life and death, past and future, faith and fear. The shipwrecks of Christmas reveal that for coastal communities, the season's joy has always been shadowed by the sea's capacity to take as well as give. From the coastal storms of 1825, which destroyed multiple vessels in a single night, to the invisible fog that sealed the fate of the Sir Redvers Buller, these maritime events demand remembrance, not only for those lost, but for what they reveal about the nature of risk, resilience, and ritual.

In commemorating these wrecks, we do more than chronicle loss, we acknowledge the lives lived at the mercy of weather and wave, the communities bound by memory and mourning, and the enduring tension between celebration and catastrophe that makes the history of Cork's Christmas coast so achingly human.

3

Memory

Memory is both the most personal and the most collective of inheritances. It survives in the quiet corners of the human mind, in shared customs, in language passed down at the hearth, and in placenames that hold stories like seeds. In this chapter, the fragments gathered under the title "Memory" are not grand historical accounts from palace steps or parliamentary halls - but something richer, more elemental: the lived experiences of ordinary people. These stories, of priests and fishwives, shipwrecks and candlelight, winters and Mass rocks, are history told from the ground up. They are the testimonies of a people who were seldom documented, but never voiceless, who held their past not in books but in hearts, tongues, and rituals.

This kind of memory is always at risk. It is transient, vulnerable to forgetting, distortion, or silence. Yet, paradoxically, it is also persistent. It clings to song, to storytelling, to seasonal habits, and to the things people do without always knowing why. In that sense, this collection is more than folklore. It is the scaffolding of historical consciousness among a people long denied the means of formal record-keeping. When institutions forget or exclude, memory steps in. It is the archive of the marginalised, and its custodians are grandmothers, blacksmiths, fishmongers, schoolchildren with notebooks, and priests like Father MacNamara, not just for their own lives, but for the lives they gathered into theirs.

The story of Father MacNamara, who features prominently in this chapter, is an embodiment of memory in action. He did not merely serve his parish; he preserved its voice. He led the building of a church, not with state funds or elite patronage, but with the small offerings of the poor; servants who had a trifle put by, farmers with coins under floorboards, community committees drawing lots to manage repayments. These acts of collective will are the marrow of social memory. They remind us that history is not only made in grand gestures but in quiet decisions, small solidarities, daily acts of giving. The building he oversaw was not just a church but a monument to cooperation, survival, and faith.

And yet, what remains of that memory is fragile. The chapel it replaced has nearly vanished; only a wall survives. The men who lifted stones are long buried. What we have are voices, faint and flickering like Christmas candles in old turnip holders. A parishioner remembers the roof going on. Another recalls the first Mass in an unfinished nave. These recollections, incomplete, imperfect, are all the more precious because of what they risk becoming: silence. Without retelling, memory dies, but in being spoken again, written down, remembered, it is rekindled.

The stories that orbit MacNamara's, tales of martyrdom, ventriloquism, midwinter shipwrecks, and sacred traditions, are just as crucial. They tell us how people lived in relation to danger, humour, belief, hunger, betrayal, and community. They preserve textures of life now hard to reconstruct, how a priest might outwit informers with theatrics, how a woman named Joan Roaster became folklore herself, how faith had to be hidden underground, in caves or whispered rituals.

There is a haunting sense of the precarious in these stories. A Mass interrupted by priest-hunters. A voice carried down a drain. A woman falling to her knees before a priest with flaming straw. These are episodes that exist at the edge of forgetting, and yet they shine with the eerie clarity that memory sometimes gives to the half-remembered. The very oddness of such details, the fresh hake that talks, ensures their survival. This is memory doing what it does best: dramatising, distilling, protecting meaning.

But memory is also bound to place. The stories here are deeply geographical. They know the names of coves, ridges, crossroads, and creeks. Poll an Bhitheamhnaigh, Cnoc an Fiolar, Ballinacubby Creek. These are not inert backdrops but living locations, storied terrains where belief, fear, and resilience intersect. To forget these stories would be to flatten the landscape itself. What is a hill without the tale of the gold buried beneath it? What is a ruined chapel without the memory of a priest murdered on Christmas Day?

Equally, memory here is seasonal. Christmas, especially, emerges as a focal point, not just a time of festivity, but a time when memory itself becomes more vivid, more insistent. The Christmas candle lit in windows, the Holy Family welcomed symbolically with food and shelter, the tragedy of deaths on snowy eves, all of these crystallise a time when light pushes back against darkness, and memory gathers, solemn and shimmering. Christmas is when memory is at its most sacred and most vulnerable.

The fragility of these traditions, and the precarious lives they record, make the act of recollection all the more urgent. This chapter is not just a gathering of tales, but a rescue, of voices that might otherwise be lost to wind and water, to silence and shame. It is memory, not as nostalgia, but as resistance. A refusal to let the stories of labourers, widows, children, and outcasts vanish into the oblivion of official history.

And so, we enter this chapter not as readers, but as inheritors. These are not quaint tales, but the foundations of identity, community, and endurance. Memory, here, is both witness and warning. It says: remember what was done, and how we endured. Remember the price of forgetting. And remember, too, the joy, the music, the jokes, the bread on the table, the candle in the window, without which survival is not enough.

Stories of Father MacNamara

When Fr Mac Namara decided to build a new church, these were the means he adopted to raise funds. He borrowed money from parishioners who had reserve cash. These included servants who had a trifle put by for the rainy day as well as farmers & traders who kept their money at home instead of lodging it in the bank. A committee of parishioners met every Sunday under the presidency of the Parish Priest, and accordingly, as subscriptions came in, lots were drawn and the lenders were repaid either in part or whole. as the amount of funds allowed.

Two Protestant benefactors helped to provide building materials. One was an ancestor of Dr Orr, occupant of the house and farm at Kilnacloona, previously occupied by Lord Kinsale, and at present by Mr John McCarthy. The other person was Mrs Dawson of Scilly who sent small boats and crews to convey the stones across the river, up the channel of Ballinacubby Creek to the quay at the end of Muddy Lane whence they were carted through Blind Gate to Friars Street. With the exception of the limestone, brought, I understand from Aherla all the material was local, and barring the stucco workers, all the mechanics were Kinsale men.

While the work was proceeding Mass continued to be celebrated in the old Chapel. I think one wall of this old Chapel still stands. In the lower part of the gable by the mortuary you can see poor rough masonry, and what looks like the jamb of a window about five feet high.

The first Mass celebrated in the new Church was the Christmas Night nine months after the laying of the foundation stone. The roof was on but the walls had yet to be plastered the galleries erected, the ornamental ceiling and window jambs to be done and the belfry to be constructed. All this work took about ten years to complete, and the new building appeared shining like a vision from the other world the people of Kinsale had reason to be proud of their Church. Apart from the pale sickly-looking strangers who moulded the figures for the centre pieces and cornices of the ceiling it was none other than Kinsale men placed in position every stone, slate, and board of that Church - even the nails were of local make - while the cost was borne exclusively by the parishioners

Apart from the building of the Church schools and Convent Fr MacNamara worked in other directions for the public good. He had a temperance society and band established in what is now known as the Ball Alley. Here he presided at monthly concerts, and in speaking to his people he reminded them that the fisherman and the labourer was as worthy of respect as the wealthiest landlord. Whenever Fr MacNamara appeared in public, he carried his parishioners with him

In 1837 Fr MacNamara and the other priests of the town attended a meeting. The candidate supported by the Catholics had won the election. A fish woman named Joan Roaster was so carried away by the enthusiasm of the hour that she dropped on her knees before the Parish Priest with a bundle of lighted straw in her canvas apron. Fr MacNamara knew this Joan Roaster well. On one occasion he saw this famous fish woman approach, marching proudly along with a losset balanced on her head and in the losset a fine hake. With Fr Mac Namara was a friend named Gallagher who could "pitch his voice" The priest whispered to Gallagher and then saluted Joan Roaster. "What sort of a fish have
you got Joan? he inquired
"A fine 'aak fresh from the say your ravarance" answered Joan, and she bent her knee.
"You're a liar, I am three weeks out of the water," said the fish. The losset and fish fell off Joan Roaster's head she screamed, clapped her hands, and, kneeling before Fr MacNamara, begged him to banish the "Ould Boy out of the 'aak"

On another occasion Fr MacNamara and his friend, the ventriloquist, were walking down Market Lane which was divided by a partly covered main drain. People hearing what they believed was the smothered cry of a child from the sewer. They raised an alarm and started tearing up the flags, but while they were working at one point the pitiful wailing of the child rose from another spot some distance away. By that time all the neighbourhood was in commotion, whereupon Fr MacNamara, fearing an accident would happen whispered to Gallagher to stop pitching his voice.[11]

---

[11] The Schools' Collection, Volume 0319, pp.243-247.

Father Downey

In the penal days there was a boy called John Downey living in Ballydonegan. One time when the soldiers came here persecuting the catholics he fled to Spain where he was educated and ordained. There was one of the O'Sullivan Beares put in his charge as the boy's parents were dead. When the boy grew up he joined the Spanish Army. After a few years in the army, he thought of visiting his native home. But Father Downey did not want to let him go as he knew the English were watching for all Catholics and that boy was a Catholic but O Sullivan persisted on going so Fr Downey came with him. They landed in Killmiciloge on the boundary between Cork and Kerry. They went from there on horse back to Finnaha and then they came across Cnoc Fuara to Coom there they remaind hiding from the English soldiers.

On Christmas night Fr Downey arranged to have a midnight Mass in Killmiciloge afew days before. Two days before Christmas a heavy shower of snow fell over all the surrounding country. On Christmas night the people were stealing away to the house in which Fr Downey was saying the Mass and a man who saw them told Puxley in Dunboy who followed the footprints in the snow to the house in which Fr Downey was saying Mass.

They hid in the wood nearby until he was alone with the boy and they they rushed in and killed him. The man who informed on him fell over a cliff in "Cnoc an Fiolar" and he was killed. The eagles ate all his body only his tongue and his hands.[12]

Collector: Máire Ní Murchadha, Allihies.
Informant: Seán Ó Murchadha, aged 85, farmer.

---

[12] The Schools' Collection, Volume 0274, pp.410-412

Má Gun

About Two hundred years ago there lived in Carn (Currane) a Robber named "Má Gun". He had a house under the ground with a very small entrance. This was very like a cave. It was in the south side of Carn hill. The name that was on this cave was Poll an Bhitheamhnaigh. This place was visited by hundreds of people every Christmas day. He used to go robbing to Kilcasken.

One day as he was comming from Kilcasken on horseback he was followed by soldiers on horseback. The soldiers overtook him. They were about to shoot him but he stopped them. He asked them to get a certain man for him but the soldiers could not find the man so they shot him. He wanted to tell the man he was looking for where his gold was but he said to no man where the gold was. He was shot on Christmas day on the north side of the hill and he was buried in the top of the hill. After some time people used to go there on Christmas day some used to try to find his gold and others to see his grave.

My Father told me this about "Má Gun". Carn hill is in my uncle's land and it was there my father grew up. He was told the story by the old people. "It is said that Má Gun threw a stone from Kinneigh, and it landed in Knockaneady (5 miles) His gold is hidden on a "bounds ditch" near a holly bush with in three fields of the public road between Carn and the Bandon river."

Collector: Mr Daniel Carey, aged 40, Curraghcrowly East.

Béaloideas

There was a man named Shean Drum - a non-Catholic and his wife a Roman Catholic living in the bottom of Kilshinahan in the time of the tyrant Moore. His wife went to Mass on Christmas day and as was customary brought home a bottle of holy water. When the dinner was on the fire, he spilled the bottle of holy water into the pot. He was a boat maker by trade. He went to a place, Ahernal in Kinsale, during the Christmas time. When the dinner was ready, they did not like not to call him in and they thought he might make a leak in the boat. He was called in and there were drinks given round. He drank the priest's good health. Then the priest asked him, "Did those words come from his heart?" "Yes," he said, "they come from my soul. If I can only understand the meaning of them." Then the priest told him to come to his house and he would give him a book to try would he believe anything and to bring back the book in a certain time. The priest waited for weeks and no reply came. Then he thought the book must have been torn and thrown in the fire. He thought of going to see him. When he reached Drum's house he asked the wife where was present, good health. Then the priest said to him did those words come from his heart "Yes" he said "they come from my soul. If I can only understand the meaning of them" Then the priest told him to come to his house and he would give him a book to try would he believe anything and to bring back the book in a certain time. The priest waited for weeks and no reply came. Then he thought the book must have been torn and thrown in the fire. He thought of going to see him. When he reached Drum's house he asked the wife where was Shean "He is below there" says she "reading" He went down and found him kneeling with bare knees on a stone, praying. The priest said to leave him alone. When he was going to Mass the Sunday after he asked two on the roadsides to sponsor him. They did and he was baptised. When Moore was passing up the road to town he met Shean and he said "Ar rugais an sagart an dhiabhal ort?" "An dearmhad" arsa Seán, Fuair sé bás 'na Sasanac agus do sgiobadh an diabhal an t-anam leis.

In the time of the "big snow" 1885 the snow reached the chimney tops. There is a story told how a man was travelling on horse-back late one day. He travelled along till he came to what he thought was a pole, or a tree, but it was the top of a chimney. He tied his horse to the chimney, and fell fast asleep on the snow. The snow melted very quickly, and next day he was found on the ground and the horse was hanging from the chimney. He wondered very much at what had happened. Other stories also indicate how high the snow was, when men fell down chimneys by making a mistake thinking they were holes in the ground.[13]

Collector: Joan O'Leary.
Informant: John O'Leary, aged 88, Skeaf.

---

[13] The Schools' Collection, Volume 0314, Page 153-157.

Story

I took down the following story as 'twas told to me. About ninety years ago the people of the Island were very very poor. A good number of families were also almost starving. At this time a Minister by the name of Spring came to the Island. He was a Kerry man and he had plenty of money. He built a school on the Island - no trace of this building today, but the site on which 'twas built is still pointed out by the old people. He also built a house which he used as a Church. He went around among the people, and offered them money and food, if they would send their children to his school, and attend service in his Church on Sundays. Most of the inhabitants were forced through poverty to accept this money and food. Those who attended his Church got plenty money and food and clothes. Others would not take either food or money and many of them died of hunger. He gave employment too to those who were willing to work and a rough road in the Midland is still known as boithrín Spring.

There was a Song made about him but I have only a couple of verses of it.

> Spring was a Kerryman born.
> He took his departure of late;
> He steered his course for Baltimore Harbour,
> And bid adieu to his old mother Kate.
> Tis there he met Carthy the Pracher (?),
> Michael Donovan, Jerry Shea then also,
> Young Harry and old Harry Casey
> And a man who they call him Joe.

Twas hard to blame the old people for turning with him, as God only knows how badly off they were; and 'twas hunger and nothing else made them do it. But plenty food came after to them.

During Spring's time a ship laden with wheat ran ashore on the Rinn Point - southern point of Island. It was on a Christmas Night, and at the dawn on Christmas morning the people went towards the wreck, and drew home the corn in strong homemade linen sheets. They ground the corn with Querns, and so they had plenty to eat then. Every one of them, except the family of McCarthy Mór Spáinneach, turned away from Spring and so he left the Island in disgust.

This McCarthy Mór died a Protestant, and one of his sons too remained a Protestant, and afterwards joined the Police Force. I met this same man afterwards when he was in the Force. His family are Protestants to this day.

Informant: Michael Mc Carthy, aged 74, Inishodriscoll.

Hollyhill

I
Sadly am I by the side of a mountain.
The lights of old Bantry are far far away.
Church bells are chiming the small hours of morning
And the search lights are looking for spies on the bay.

Chorus
Sandy and Jack they rolled home together
A nice Christmas motto hung up on the wall.
"Look up" says Jack Murphy to his friend Alexander
"And read for yourself happy welcomes to all."

II
I fancy. I see the home Christmas candles
And hear the greetings of mother to welcome me back
I fancy, I see the home Christmas candles
lighting the way of the wanderer Jack.

III
Cursed Hollyhill, I know you're enchanted
The moon in its beams refuses to shine.
Where are the stars, are they all immigrated
Out in the trenches where volunteers line.

IV
Lonely am I by the side of a mountain
Seeking my cabin so lonely and rude.
The man who will guide me, I'll treat him to Whiskey
That was bought at O Driscolls the pub by the mill.

This song was written by a man named Jack Murphy who lived in Hollyhill, in the year nineteen seventeen. On Christmas night of that year, he was going home from Bantry, he was very intoxicated, and he lost his way on the hillside. He fell, and a man named Sandy Lannan came that way and took him home, and afterwards Murphy composed that song.[14]

Collected at Inchiclogh.

---

[14] The Schools' Collection, Volume 0284, pp.220-221.

Local Happenings in Ballydesmond

There are no local happenings of any concern in the parish of Ballydesmond since the times of the "Black and Tans" were uncontrollable and one day whilst in this mood they entered the Village of Ballydesmond after a local ambush and burned three houses. Mr. McAuliffes, Mr Vaughan's, and Mr. Ó Sullivan's Post Office and also subjected some of the civil population to very harsh treatment.

Years previous to that there was a very sad occurrence near the village of Gneeveguilla. A bog moved and ran into the lakes near Killarney carrying in its way the whole of the Donnelly Family with the exception of one girl who at the time of the occurrence was visiting a friend in Mocha, near Ballydesmond. There was also carried two cows. They were found later on near Killarney with an infant that was sleeping in a cradle when it was taken.

This was a very sad occurrence as they were taken wholly unawares in the dead of night never expecting such a calamity approaching the Christmas festival as the local poet put it then.

> The joys of Christmas ringing.
> Round their little humble cot,
> But Ere the morning it had come,
> It proved a treacherous spot.

A little while before the Black and Tan regime this country was badly infected with the flu so much so that a great many people died of various ages. The only ones to escape infection were mostly children under eight years.

Doctors then could not prescribe a cure in time to save the patients with the result that the death used occur in a period of three or four days.[15]

Informant: John O'Connor, Age: 55 Ballydesmond.

---

[15] The Schools' Collection, Volume 359, pp.35-37.

Penal Times near Berrings

At Carrig-an-Aifrinn near Berrings mass used be celebrated in Penal times. A priest 30 yrs old just arrived from Rome, was saying Mass one Christmas morning and at the moment of Consecration a company of priest hunters came up and murdered him at the altar.

Tradition says the tolling of a bell used to be heard every Christmas morning up to 1916.[16]

Collector: Mary O Callaghan, Agharinagh.
Informant: Edmond O Callaghan.

Reflections

Memory, as gathered in this chapter, does not arrive as a straight line, nor as fixed truth. It comes to us like candlelight through frosted glass, flickering, partial, but illuminating. In these recollections of faith and frost, of shipwreck and resistance, of humour, hunger, and holy days, we find not only echoes of the past, but blueprints for understanding the richness and the risk of memory itself. These stories endure not because they are grand, but because they are human. They show us that memory is both fragile and ferocious, easily lost, yet stubborn in its will to survive.

The people remembered in these pages, Father MacNamara, Joan Roaster, Father Downey, Má Gun, the children lighting candles in turnips, were not national figures. Their names appear in no textbooks. Yet they stand at the centre of a different kind of history: one told from the hearth, the field, the altar stone in the woods. This is bottom-up history, recorded not with ink on parchment but with voice, passed from mouth to ear, mother to child, parishioner to pupil. And because it was passed like this, it bears the marks of the human: tenderness, bias, gaps, humour, fear, invention.

These marks are not imperfections. They are the very soul of folklore. For folklore is not merely a poor cousin of history, it is its counterweight. Where history seeks to formalise and freeze, memory resists, shapeshifting and breathing across generations. And in doing so, it preserves something precious: the emotional truths of a community. These truths often outlast facts. We may forget dates, but we remember the voice that said, "You're a liar, I'm three weeks out of the water." We remember

---

[16] The Schools' Collection, Volume 0348, Page 220

the man who gave his life to say Mass in a snowbound glen. We remember the child who tied a horse to a chimney.

In this way, memory becomes not just a record but a relationship. It connects us not just to events, but to people, to their humour, their faith, their fears, their resourcefulness. We feel for them, not because we know every detail, but because we recognise ourselves in the fragments. The loss of a priest, the light of a Christmas candle, the need to laugh even amid hunger, these resonate because they are still true. They remind us that memory does not fade when its subjects die, but when we stop telling their stories.

And yet, even as we cherish memory, we must also acknowledge its precarity. These stories survived because someone bothered to tell them. To write them down. To remember. Without that effort, often unpaid, unsung, and unseen, they would have dissolved into silence. That is the task of every generation: to carry forward what matters, even when it risks being lost in translation. To recognise that history is not only what happened, but what we choose to remember.

There is something poignant in how many of these stories revolve around Christmas, a time when the line between sacred and domestic thins, and memory feels closer, more alive. At Christmas, people remember who is gone. They perform rituals without fully knowing why. They leave a light in the window. They lay out bread and butter. These are gestures of hospitality, but also of remembrance. They say, "You are still welcome here. You are not forgotten." In this way, the people in these stories, and the tellers who followed them, remind us that memory is love made visible.

What we learn from this chapter is that memory is never just about the past. It is always about what we choose to carry forward. The figures here, priests and poets, outlaws and mourners, are not just subjects of curiosity. They are ancestors of meaning. Their stories are part of the long braid that binds Ireland's people to their land, their language, and one another.

To remember them is not to indulge nostalgia, but to resist erasure. In a world increasingly shaped by speed, amnesia, and disconnection, these old stories call us back to slowness, to place, to care. They remind us that memory is an act of attention. And that attention, in turn, is a form of honour.

So let us keep telling them. Let us light the candle. Let us name the places. Let us listen for the voice in the stone or the drain. Let us remember, not because the past was perfect, but because without memory, we are unmoored.

These words, then, are not a conclusion. They are an invitation. To listen more closely. To cherish more deeply. To remember more fully. For in remembering them, we remember ourselves.

4

Faith and Superstition

In Ireland, the line between faith and superstition has always been fine, at times invisible, and often walked with reverence, fear, and inherited certainty. Especially in the country's rural heartlands, one finds a world in which prayers are whispered in chapels and charms are muttered under breath, where the Virgin Mary and the banshee might be invoked with equal sincerity. This duality, this cultural layering, is not a contradiction in Irish tradition but a kind of cohabitation, centuries-deep and seasonally heightened around the feast days of the liturgical year, none more so than at Christmas.

This chapter explores the enduring entanglement between Christian faith and folklore-based superstition in Ireland, through personal testimonies, stories, and customs gathered from the National Folklore Collection archives. These testimonies come not from the high pulpits or scholarly journals but from the kitchens and fields of ordinary people, where belief was lived rather than theorised. Here, Christmas becomes the key lens, a time when the sacred and the spectral press close, when holy rites, folk warnings, and otherworldly presences are all understood to coexist in the season's long, dark nights.

To understand this entanglement, we must first understand what is meant by faith and superstition. Faith, in the Irish Catholic tradition, is structured and sacramental: it is the doctrine of the Church, the worship of God, the celebration of feast days, and the transmission of grace through prayer, fasting, and holy rites. Superstition, by contrast, is unofficial, intuitive, inherited orally, unlicensed knowledge that deals with the unseen and unpredictable. It is the milk left out for the fairies, the whispered charm against the evil eye, or passing a fairy fort.

But to divide these neatly is to miss the way they were, and often still are, entwined. Superstition did not necessarily undermine faith in Ireland, it shadowed and supported it. It filled in the gaps where official theology offered no comfort, where doctrine met doubt, grief, fear, or wonder. Faith was communal and taught from the altar; superstition was local and remembered in the home. Together, they offered a total cosmology.

When Christianity arrived in Ireland in the fifth century, it absorbed rather than erased some native belief systems. Celtic traditions, steeped in seasonal rituals, spirits of place, and sacred trees, were not dismantled so much as reinterpreted. Wells dedicated to pagan deities were rechristened in the names of saints. Imbolc became St. Brigid's Day; Samhain became All Souls'. Sacred groves became sites for Mass rocks during the Penal era. Over time, this fusion formed a distinctly Irish Catholicism, rich in ritual, heavy with inherited awe, and shaped by centuries of oral tradition and colonial resistance.

At Christmastime, this hybridity is especially visible. Catholic doctrine marks the season with vigils, Midnight Masses, the Nativity, and Twelve Days of solemn celebration. But Irish Christmas customs often echo older, folkloric ideas about spirits, the dead, and the threshold between worlds. It is at Christmas, for example, that animals are said to kneel in their stalls at midnight, just as they did in Bethlehem. It is then that ghosts walk the land, the fairies are active, and candles burn in windows to guide both Christ and the wandering dead. There are tales of phantom Masses said by dead priests, of flickering lights over graves, of donkeys bearing the mark of Christ for their role in the Nativity. These are not mere inventions, but expressions of a belief world in which the divine and the uncanny coexisted.

In the testimonies presented here, we encounter this world in vivid detail. A robin, bloodied by its compassion for Christ, earns its red breast. A blackthorn tree blooms in winter to shelter the Holy Family. A poor man hears a ghostly Mass said by a long-dead priest. In another tale, a miser's skeleton reassembles itself on Christmas night to reveal hidden gold. These stories contain moral instruction, seasonal memory, communal values, and a blurred boundary between religious reverence and mythic imagination.

Importantly, many of these stories do not distinguish clearly between "faith" and "superstition." A priest's ghost is just as real as the living celebrant of the Mass. Fairies and the souls of the dead are treated with respect alongside the Holy Family. The presence of relics, sacred trees, and animal omens coexist with the performance of the rosary and the sacrament of Communion. The same household might prepare a Christmas table in honour of Christ and leave food for the Good People, just in case.

This layered belief system is particularly intense in times of hardship. In Ireland's long-nineteenth century of poverty, eviction, emigration, and famine, the official rites of the Church offered comfort, but they did not always answer the needs of the soul. Folk practices provided accessible ways to channel grief, express hope, or explain misfortune. A dead relative might warn you of danger. A candle might guide a soul home. A red thread might protect your baby when prayers alone felt insufficient.

Moreover, Christmas was not just a time of joy but of anxiety. The turning of the year, the long nights, the frozen fields, all lent themselves to stories of ghosts, visions, and second sight. Just as nature lay still, the veil between the living and the dead was believed to thin. Thus, Christmas became a season of spiritual double vision: joy at the birth of Christ and unease at the forces abroad in the dark. In many households, especially in remote areas, the two could not be separated.

And while the Church often condemned superstitious practices, it also recognised their cultural persistence. Priests themselves sometimes featured in such stories, offering penance from beyond the grave, appearing to guide the faithful, or being seen as protectors in life and beyond. In Irish tradition, the figure of the priest is both shepherd and potential folk hero, a bearer of sacrament but also a guardian against ill fortune.

The tension between ecclesiastical authority and local belief shaped how customs were passed down. While the Church urged uniformity, Irish religiosity remained variegated. Faith was practiced through Mass and confession, but also through lore, legend, and household ritual. The stories presented in this chapter are the echoes of that layered faith: rich, mysterious, and unbothered by theological consistency.

In bringing these stories together, this chapter is not simply recording old customs. It is listening to a worldview, a way of living that sees no contradiction in a crib adorned with holly, a Mass served by a ghost, and a robin as Christ's tiny companion. It is a world where the miraculous, the mythic, and the mundane dwell side by side. It is, in short, an Irish Christmas.

Christmas services in Cork could draw extraordinary crowds, and the chapels, often small, poorly ventilated, and already stretched by poverty and population growth, were seldom designed for the pressure placed upon them during the festive season. The desire to attend early Mass or midnight devotions meant that Catholics packed into galleries and aisles long before dawn, creating a living sense of communal warmth, but also real physical risk.

A grim reminder of this occurred on Christmas Day in Bandon, when an overcrowded Roman Catholic chapel became the scene of sudden panic. One of the long wooden forms in the gallery collapsed without warning, and a cry went up that the entire structure was giving way. In an instant the congregation surged towards the exits. People were seen leaping from the gallery into the aisle and even through the chapel windows into the street. In the confusion that followed, many were injured, limbs were broken, and at least six people were crushed to death in the struggle to escape. Windows, doors, and railings gave way beneath the force of the crowd, leaving the building badly damaged.

Events such as this, while mercifully rare, reveal how central communal worship was to Christmas in Cork. Even fear, cold, darkness, and cramped conditions did not deter people from attending. Faith, devotion, and the powerful magnetism of the season brought communities together in numbers that could strain the very buildings meant to shelter them. The tragedy at Bandon stands as a stark testament to the intensity of Christmas observance in nineteenth-century Cork, where the pull of early Mass was strong enough to fill chapels beyond safe capacity.

Festivals of the Year

There are a great many feasts in the year, but Christmas is by far the most joyful of all. It falls on the twenty-fifth day of December and it also commemorates the Birth of Our Lord Jesus Christ. Christmas is the time of joy for young and old. All the young children gather their pennies together to buy little presents that they see on the windows. All the windows are decorated with holly, ivy, coloured electric bulbs, and of course toys for the young children to buy. They all look forward to Santa Claus bringing them a lot of toys. Every priest says a mass on Christmas Day. After Christmas Day comes St. Stephen's Day. It falls on the 26th of December. All the grown up boys go all over the town and country gathering money to bury the wren with high fiddles on their faces on that day.[17]

Informant: Dan Moynihan, Millstreet, Co. Cork

---

[17] The Schools' Collection, Volume 0323, p.357.

Christmas Day

Christmas Day is the most joyous and merry time of the whole year even though it occurs in the dreary winter. On the first Christmas morning Our Lord was born and that is the reason there is such joy in every heart. On this great day of days everybody is up earlier than usual so that they will be in time for Mass. When breakfast is over everybody goes to mass and receives Holy Communion and pays a visit to the Crib that day. We were leaving for Mass at 8.15 a.m. When we went into the chapel, we went in to see the crib and to pray to Our Lord. The crib was decorated with holly and ivy. On returning from Mass, we had the Christmas dinner. The twelve days between 20th December and the 6th January are called Christmas or Yuletide. Nations and countries have different customs.

In this locality people think it is right to let the door open on Christmas Eve. Other people say that this is only superstition. In this locality and I dare say everywhere the people have a roast turkey or goose according to their means for their dinner on Christmas Day.
They also have a plum pudding. Every house is decorated with red berried holly and ivy and mistletoe.

Christmas is a time of joy and merrymaking and feasting. During the days of Christmas ghosts are supposed to be seen frequently whether it is true or not I do not know. On Christmas morning there are two Masses in Araglin and three in Kilworth. I went to nine o'clock Mass in Araglin. Most people who have the opportunity received Holy Communion on Christmas morning in honour of the birth of Christ. On Christmas Eve night the children hang up their stockings in expectation of Santa Claus to come and fill them with good things.[18]

---

[18] The Schools' Collection, Volume 0377, p.064.

Legends of the Holy Family

This is the story of how the robin got its red breast. It is said that when Our lord was crowned with thorns a robin came and tried to take the thorns from His Head and some blood got on its breast and since that day it is red.

There is another story also how the robin got its red breast. It is said that when the Jews were crucifying Our Lord that the robin tried to pull out the nails from His hands when He was dying. A drop of blood fell on the breast of the robin and ever since that day it has a red breast.

This is the story of how the donkey got the cross on its back. The first one is that when Our Lord was going in to Jerusalem he had no animal to ride ans some person gave him a present of a donkey. As a reward for the donkey's good work Our Lord put a cross on its back and since that day there is a cross on the donkey's back.

When the Holy Family were making their flight into Egypt it began to rain one night and they had no shelter only a blackthorn bush without without leaves or blossoms. During the night they were very comfortable and when they awoke in the morning the bush was covered with blossoms and leaves. Since that day the blackthorn bush blossoms first every year.

When Our Lord was born Christmas night in the stable at Bethlehem, he had no bed only a bit of.hay to sleep on in the manger. There was an ox and an ass in the stable. He had only a small bit of hay and the ass ate some of it but the cow refused to eat it. She kept Our Lord warm with her breath. Ever since that night the donkey has to do all the hard work while the ox has a fine life. It is also said that on every Christmas night the ass and the ox go on their knees on Christmas night at twelve o'clock to commemorate the night Our Lord was born.

When Our Lord was in the cave on Christmas night the mouth of the cave was closed by two plants holly and ivy and they protected Our Lord from the cold wind and ever since the cribs in the Catholic churches are covered with holly and ivy.[19]

Collector: Mr Con Lucey, Subulter, Co. Cork
Informant: Mr John Sheehan, Ballygrady North, Co. Cork

---

[19] The Schools' Collection, Volume 0364, pp.343-344.

A Story About the Holy Family

There are a few stories told locally about the Holy Family. One story is as follows. When the Holy Family were fleeing from Herod's soldiers, they met men sowing corn. These men gave them food and drink. Just then the corn which they had sown sprung up. On the following day when the reapers were reaping the corn Herod's soldiers came enquiring of them if they had seen a man woman and infant pass along that way. The workmen told them that they had seen them pass when they were sowing the seed. When the soldiers heard this, they thought that they were on the wrong path. They were just in the act of turning back when a Dearg Daol [devils' coach-horse beetle] in its peculiar creaking noise said "indé" [tomorrow] thus informing the soldiers that the Holy Family were not far before them. Then the soldiers went on hot pursuit. For that reason, people never like the Dearg Daol. When people see it, they kill it. When old people see it, they make the sign of the cross seven times on it. Then they say "Mo pheacaí ort [My sins on you]" and then they kill it.[20]

Collector: Nora Sullivan, Annagannihy.
Informant: Mr Michael Sullivan.

---

[20] The Schools' Collection, Volume 341, Page 71-72.

The Miser's Treasure

Once there was a very wealthy man who was a great miser. At length he died. They searched all the castle in search of his great fortune but there was no trace of it to be found. But every Christmas evening the ghost of the man would walk around the castle and look at it. The people said that they would not live in the castle at all because they said they thought that it was haunted. But a poor sailor that was living near the castle took courage. He said he would live in the castle, and he did. On Christmas night when he was cooking sausages in the frying pan, a bone fell down the chimney, then another and t another till all the bones of a man were there. Then they all joined and shaped themselves into a man who told the sailor to follow him, and he took him down to a dungeon where all his wealth was.[21]

Informant: Hazel Bird, Age: 11, Maryfield.

---

[21] The Schools' Collection, Volume 0314, p.67.

A Christmas Morning Experience - Circa 1867 or 1870

Our little house stood on a bleak mountain a considerable distance from any other dwelling. In front of the door was a large rough field or rather common which to our recollection had never been tilled or fenced. The locality was very sparsely populated but people believed that in olden times the land had supported very many more dwellers than at the time of my story.

It was on a Christmas morning. The whole family had arisen very early by candlelight to prepare for the journey to early morning Mass. The head of the household had opened the door and gone outside for some purpose when unusual sounds apparently coming from the open common attracted his attention. He heard shouts, sounds of running, and blows that usually accompany the game of hurling. He was amazed and dashed in to inform the household. The father mother and all the family came outside, and standing together that still Christmas morning, heard the sounds of struggling panting players in action, shouts of encouragement from supporters, and all the hurly burly of an exciting game. It used to come up quite close at times as the game, progressed. None of the family saw anything though all were staring at the playing pitch. As they still stood and listened, fascinated, there came a lull in the play, and then -ringing clear in the morning air - they heard a voice clear as a silver bell enquire "Did the bell ring yet?"[22]

Collected at Drinagh, Co. Cork

---

[22] The Schools' Collection, Volume 0303, p.425-426.

Story

In my uncle's land in Scarteen, about two miles north of Newmarket, there is a field, and in the middle of this there is a tree known as the Chalice Tree. When this tree blooms each year, the blossoms are of a rich, red colour. It has a long, straight stem and it is shaped like a chalice; therefore, it gets the name from this. A poor woman who lives near this place sent her son years ago to gather brosna and he gathered up a bundle of sticks together with a piece of a branch from the Chalice Tree and went for home. When he came to the first fence, he could not cross it, no matter how he tried. He remained there for some time until his mother came to call him. She asked him what delayed him, "Mother," he said, "I can't cross the fence!" "Jim," she said, "did you interfere in any way with the Tree of the Chalice?" "Oh," he said. "I took a piece of a branch from off the tree." "Go, as quickly as you can," she said, and put it back again". The boy did so, and it grew without a root, just where he stuck it in the ground near the Chalice Tree.

Adjoining this field is a smaller field where two graves are to be seen and in it there grows a sycamore tree. It grows up to a height of six feet or so in one straight stem and then it opens out into two branches growing straight to a height of nine or ten feet. At the trunk of the print of a horse's hoof, and fetlock, can easily be seen. A few years ago, my uncle was ploughing that field and he found a dagger under the ground. It is said that a Mass Rock was situated a few miles from this, nearer to Meelin. During the Penal Times a priest who was celebrating Mass got word from the scouts who were watching for him, and his fellow priest, that Cromwell's soldiers were on their track and they ran with the chalice to this field and hid it before they were cruelly murdered by Cromwell's soldiers. The graves are said to be those of the two priests who were murdered by Cromwell's soldiers. Up to nine or ten years ago it is said that each Christmas night candles could be seen lighting and the form of a priest praying near the tree. Several priests and people visit this field to see the remarkable Chalice Tee, and the Sycamore Trees, and the graves.[23]

Collector: Eíbhlís Ních Amhlaoibh.
Informant: Miss Mollie Mc Auliffe, Glennamucklagh East.

---

[23] The Schools' Collection, Volume 0351, pp.332-334.

A Folk Tale of Riverstown House

All day long the snow had been falling and the ground was covered with a thick white carpet but inside Riverstown House the log fire crackled cheerfully and the dancing flames threw weird shadows on the rich tapestried walls. It was Christmas Eve and also marked the coming of age of Sir John McCarthy Moore the only son of his widowed mother. The guests were seated around the fire, among them the dark eyed Spanish girl to whom Sir John was shortly to be married. Someone suggested telling a ghost story. Sir John said that there was a haunted room in the house where one of his ancestors was murdered. The room was locked and never used, the servants being afraid to go in its vicinity. Sir John's cousin, Peter, who was a daredevil suggested visiting the room just for curiosity. Lady McCarthy Moore at once implored her son not to go but his Spanish lady who loved adventure dared him to go. His mother's entreaties were in vain, and she was forced to give up the key. Sir John and Peter were to sleep there for the night notwithstanding the remonstrates of the guests. Next morning, one by one, the guests appeared at breakfast but no sight of the two adventurers. One of the guests, a doctor, no longer able to contain his anxiety, went to find them. One knocking at the door he received no answer, so he called for some help and with the aid of a hatchet he at length succeeded in breaking down the door. The sight which met his eyes to put it mildly stunned him. Stretched across the bed fully clothed lay the dead body of the baronet while crouching in the corner was Peter a gibbering idiot. No one ever solved this mystery.[24]

Collector: Patricia Nyhan, Glanmore.
Informant: Ellen Coleman.

---

[24] The Schools' Collection, Volume 0389, pp.432-433.

Additional Fairy Stories

Fairy stories in this district are related about two kinds of fairies - Good People who come to warn people of danger or help them in need and Sprits who were harmful and who injured people.

Good People were usually the souls of one's nearest relatives. They are supposed to come back to help sometimes. Mrs Leahy of Castle Island - a widow - relates a story to prove this. "One night" she says, "she heard her husband call her three times in succession. The voice came from outside the house. Mrs Leahy was afraid to go out.

When morning came, she rose quickly and went out believing that something must be wrong. She went to the cow house and found that one of her cows had calved during the night, and to her surprise she found the calf had been taken and put on a little bundle of hay well away from the cow. Mrs Leahy believes it was one of the Good People did it.

To show their gratitude and love for these Good People, food is left on the table for them at night especially on Christmas Night when the table is laid with cloth, cups, and food of all kinds.

People also think that when milk, tea, or any food is spilled that it is the fairies have need of it and so they used say in Irish after spilling something, "Sláinte go ndéarna, Má bhí éinne 'na ghádhtar. [Health to anyone in need]."[25]

---

[25] The Schools' Collection, Volume 1128, pp.75-76.

Reverend William O Shea – Parish Priest, Schull

The following interesting account of the folklore of this district has been supplied by Seumas Breathnach Cionn tSáile. He wrote this down from the old people upwards of thirty years ago.

Rev. Wm. O'Shea was a native of Tracton Parish and died P.P. of Schull 20th April 1823 and was buried there.

Late on the following Christmas Eve a man named Tomás na Hoola was standing on the bridge at Minane when the spirit of the dead priest stood before him. Tomás on seeing the apparition tried to move away, until the priest assured him that he was in no danger and also asked the man to listen carefully to what he the priest was about to say.

The priest went on to say that his coffin was swimming in water and that it was his desire to have the remains removed from Schull to the burial place of his parents at Temple Brigid, (Crosshaven, Co. Cork.) He further said that the friends who would volunteer to remove his remains would find their task an easy one. They would go by boat, of course, and on their voyage to the west they would be invisible, as their craft would be covered with a mist. Tomás asked for a sign, and it was given. On entering the public house at the corner then kept by one of the O'Sheas, brother to the priest, and later by Matty MacDonnell, a dog would take the Christmas candle off and would sit on the floor holding it between his paws. This happened, whereupon Tomás conveyed the message from the dead priest to all the friends.

At that time several farmers on the seaboard of Tracton Parish had fishing hookers and were all acquainted with the coast of West Cork. A crew set out for Schull inspected the grave of Fr. O'Shea and made arrangements for a second trip.

Soon after a party of five men set out in a boat belonging to Ahern of Fountainstown. The crew comprised the owner of the craft (Matt Ahern), Mick Sullivan, (carpenter of Minane Bridge grandfather of Seán a' Gabha), the brother of the priest, and two others named Farrissey and Jeffers. Besides provision for the voyage, they took towed to the boat a sheaf of wheat in which they stuck a lighted blessed candle. The voyage to Schull was short and uneventful and on pulling ashore they proceeded to open the grave, lift the coffin and place it aboard the hooker. Scarcely was this done when natives discovered what was afoot, an alarm was raised, and an attempt made to seize the strangers. But no boat could be manned in time to pursue the Ringabella craft. Even if a pursuing boat could be got it would be of no use as a fog enveloped the boat from the east. All that the men of Schull could do was to hurl stones out into the sea. The

Ringabella boat with the coffin of the priest aboard glided homewards without much help from the crew. Some of the voyagers fell asleep and were roused by the shock of the keel striking ground. Unknown to themselves they had come ashore at Ringabella.[26]

Collector: Seumas Breathnach, Kinsale.
Informant: Patsy Shea, Oyster Haven, a member of the same family as the priest.

A Burning Bush at Ballacummer Bridge

A man from the Ballineen district was returning from Clonakilty one winter's night. When he reached Ballacummer Bridge he saw a bush burning on the road. He took it as a joke on the part of some parties returning from a "sgoruíocht". Suddenly it died out and a huge dog appeared. Its eyes were like blazing coals and it ran about the cart barking. The horse refused to move and began to tremble all over and the man was so much afraid that he couldn't do anything. After some time the horse moved again and the dog followed behind the cart for about a quarter of a mile and then disappeared. Next morning the horse was found dead in the stable and the owner was taken ill and remained in bed for several weeks.[27]

Collected by Liam Ó Ruairc, Knockskagh.
Informant: Randal Ó Muirthille, Ballyvahallig Crossroads.

---

[26] The Schools' Collection, Volume 321, pp.148-150.
[27] The Schools' Collection, Volume 0311, p.417.

The Priest's Penance

One winter's evening a poor man was walking along a country road. Night was falling & he had got no lodgings. Soon he came on to the country chapel which was in a very lonely place & he went in to say a few prayers. In the meantime, the chapel man who took care of the chapel & the grounds came on and locked the door.

When the poor man had finished his prayers, he went to the door in order to go out. But he found it was locked. He tried to go out through an open window, but it was too high a jump, so he had to remain inside.

He stretched on one of the seats and fell asleep. About midnight he heard somebody speak so he got up and looked round. He saw a priest on the altar but no server. The priest asked, "Is there anybody here to serve mass?" But the poor old man was too frightened to answer. The priest asked again but got no answer. Finally, he went back to the sacristy.

The old man was weak with shock and fright, and he made no delay in the chapel when it was opened the following day. During the day he told his story to another friend he met. The friend was very surprised but asked him why he hadn't answered. They decided to go back again that night & watch proceedings.

Just at the stroke of twelve that night a priest came out. They had never seen him before. Though the friend was a very brave man still he felt his hair stand on end. All the same when he heard "Is there anybody here to serve mass" he had enough courage to say "Yes". The priest said, "Come here". They both approached the altar. The priest gave them a prayer book & began mass They served him as they did their own priests in their youth. When mass was over, he turned to them & said. "I'm alright now. You can go. I have been here for many years waiting for a living person to serve my mass but until now I've found none. But now I'm happy," And so saying he disappeared. The two were very surprised but they slept soundly in the chapel till next day & then took their departure.[28]

---

[28] The Schools' Collection, Volume 0318, pp.107-108.

A Shared Hearth

As the last candle flickers on the Christmas windowsill and the fire dies low in the hearth, what remains in the stories we've just read is not simply the echo of forgotten customs or quaint superstitions. What lingers is a deep truth about the Irish imagination, a truth forged in the interweaving of faith and folklore, the sacred and the uncanny. These stories, customs, and rituals, far from being just remnants of a bygone era, speak to a way of seeing the world where the divine and the mysterious are not distant concepts but intimate presences.

`Faith and superstition in Ireland were not opposing systems, they were parallel ways of understanding. At times they clashed, certainly, and ecclesiastical authorities often sought to separate doctrinal truth from what they saw as pagan survivals or ignorant habits. But in the lived experience of many Irish people, particularly in rural areas, these two strands of belief wove tightly together. The world was populated not just by saints and angels but by fairies and spirits; not just by doctrine but by stories; not just by the Mass but by signs, symbols, and seasonal warnings.

Christmas exemplifies this duality in its purest form. It is the holiest of feasts, marked by liturgy, the Nativity story, and the central mystery of the Incarnation. Yet it is also the season when ghosts appear on castle stairs, when animals kneel at midnight, when the dead say Mass, and when the wind might carry a warning cry across the bog. Faith gives Christmas its structure, Mass, prayers, the celebration of Christ's birth. But superstition gives it its texture, the fear, the wonder, the belief in things unseen. One offers stability, the other invites awe.

This layering of belief is not accidental, nor is it unique to Ireland. But what makes the Irish example so compelling is how deeply these beliefs remain embedded in story and landscape. A tree is not just a tree, it is the Chalice Tree, said to bloom from priestly martyrdom. A robin is not just a bird, it is marked by Christ's blood. A cow's refusal to eat hay becomes a sign of divine grace. The stories are hyper-local, often set in specific fields or near known landmarks, yet they echo universal themes: sacrifice, protection, betrayal, divine presence, and supernatural justice.

Superstition has often been treated dismissively, as a symptom of ignorance or backwardness. But when we view it through the lens of oral culture and symbolic meaning, we find it to be a form of ancestral logic. It is, in essence, a language of survival and meaning-making. It allows people to explain misfortune, to give reverence to nature, to build memory into landscape. A ghost in a chapel is not just a tale to frighten children; it is a meditation on penance, memory, and the unfinished business of the soul.

The belief that the dead return on Christmas night, or that a donkey kneels in the stable at midnight, might not stand up to scientific scrutiny, but that is not the point. These beliefs create continuity between the living and the dead, between humans and animals, between past and present. They affirm that Christmas is not only about the birth of one child long ago but about the eternal recurrence of mystery and light in a dark world.

This cohabitation of faith and superstition is also about presence, the idea that spiritual forces are close at hand. In the testimonies shared, spirits speak, fairies intervene, and divine signs appear in humble things. There is no rigid divide between heaven and earth. The sacred is not confined to church walls or theological texts; it pulses through the rhythms of daily life. The laying of food for spirits on Christmas Eve, the prayers for dead priests, the fear of the Dearg Daol, all reflect a worldview where the material and spiritual overlap constantly.

There is also a profound emotional honesty in these stories. They acknowledge that belief is not always tidy or consistent. A person might attend three Masses on Christmas Day, then still kill a beetle believed to betray the Holy Family. A poor family might decorate the crib with ivy and holly out of reverence, and also leave bread on the table for the "Good People." These are not contradictions; they are expressions of layered belief systems passed down through generations. People acted not out of rigid dogma but out of habit, inheritance, intuition, and reverence.

In this way, superstition and faith often served the same emotional needs: to protect, to explain, to connect. When a ghost knocks at the door on Christmas night, or a priest's spirit returns to request a Mass, these stories carry the emotional weight of grief, memory, and unfinished prayer. They express a longing for the eternal, for contact, for redemption. And that, ultimately, is what faith offers too: not just belief in the invisible, but trust that the invisible holds meaning.

Perhaps the most important takeaway from these stories is that they were communal. They were told aloud, around fires, in schools, in farm kitchens. They were shared across generations and shaped by local memory. Even the supernatural events are rarely solitary. There is almost always a witness: a father, a neighbour, a sailor, a priest, a child. This underscores the social role of belief. Faith and superstition were not just private convictions, they were woven into the very structure of Irish rural life. They were how communities processed death, misfortune, joy, and change.

Of course, much of this has changed. Ireland today is far more urban, secular, and globally connected than it was even a century ago. The authority of the Church has waned; belief in fairies and ghostly Masses may seem like relics of another time. And yet the emotional logic of these stories continues to resonate. People still light candles in windows at Christmas. They still tell stories about haunted places and signs from the dead. The impulse to honor the unseen, to mark time with ritual, to find meaning in nature and mystery, these persist, even if the forms have evolved.

In commemorating these stories now, we do not need to take every word literally to value them. Their power lies not in factual accuracy but in symbolic richness. They remind us that for many generations of Irish people, faith was not just something recited from a catechism, and superstition was not merely irrational fear. Both were ways of making sense of a world that was often harsh, beautiful, and mysterious.

Faith and superstition shared the same landscape, the same hearth. One brought comfort in the pews, the other in the fields and shadows. Both helped people feel less alone. Both offered stories to explain what could not otherwise be explained. Both shaped how Irish people prepared for, experienced, and remembered Christmas.

To understand Ireland's past, and to feel its spiritual texture today, we must listen to both voices: the voice of the priest at the altar and the voice of the old woman whispering a charm; the story told at Mass and the story told at the fireside. Between them lies the fullness of a people's soul.

5

Traditions

In every culture, traditions act as living bridges, spanning generations, grounding identity, and giving rhythm to life. In rural Ireland, and particularly in County Cork, traditions are not just old habits or quaint customs. They are expressions of faith, folklore, and family. This chapter, titled simply *"Traditions"*, explores how the people of Cork have preserved, transformed, and passed down the customs of Christmas, a season imbued with meaning, memory, and ritual. Through these enduring practices, Cork's communities demonstrate how tradition offers not only continuity, but a way of understanding the world, celebrating together, and honouring the sacred.

Across the testimonies collected in townlands and parishes, from Ballyhea to Bere Island, from Drimoleague to Macroom, a portrait emerges of a people for whom Christmas is the beating heart of the year. While rooted in Christian belief, the festival is also shaped by centuries-old pre-Christian and folkloric rituals. The traditions surrounding Christmas in Cork are distinctive: some deeply solemn, others joyful and rowdy, but all echoing a reverence for community, home, and shared experience.

A central element of Cork's Christmas traditions is preparation, not just materially, but spiritually. Houses are whitewashed and adorned with holly and ivy, evergreen plants, long associated with protection and renewal. These are not mere decorations, but symbolic gestures tying the present to the past. Each leaf and berry hung in doorways or around the hearth speaks to an Irish tradition where nature and the divine were always intertwined.

The Christmas candle, often placed in the front window, becomes a beacon of faith and welcome. In some homes, it is lit by the youngest in the house; in others, by the family patriarch. The act is usually accompanied by a prayer or blessing, one particularly touching example is the wish "that we may all be alive this time twelve months." In this simple act lies the essence of tradition: it remembers, it hopes, and it connects.

Meals, too, carry the weight of tradition. On Christmas Eve, many families eat stockfish with butter and milk, a nod to the older Catholic fast days. This modest meal is a spiritual preparation for the richness of Christmas Day, when tables are filled with turkey, goose, plum pudding, and every available delicacy, no matter how poor the household. One tradition recorded describes two suppers: potatoes, and fish early in the evening, and tea with cakes later. These shared meals bind families together not just through food, but through storytelling, song, and memory.

But tradition in Cork is not confined to the sacred or the somber. Joyful mischief and pageantry have their place, most famously in the Wren Boys, who take over the countryside each St Stephen's Day. From dawn till dark, boys and men dress in comic disguises, masks, and ribbons. Carrying a holly bush supposedly holding a hunted wren, they travel from house to house, singing, playing instruments, and collecting money. The tradition is theatrical, humorous, and full of local pride, but also steeped in older symbolism. The wren, the "king of all birds," may once have represented sacrifice or the old year dying away. Its place in Cork's living folklore reveals how traditions adapt but never lose their resonance.

Numerous variations of the Wren tradition exist across Cork and variations of the Wren song are presented here. In the hunt for a real wren was once central to the ritual, while in Liscarroll or Ballyhea, boys substituted moss and ribbon for the bird. The songs they sang varied too, though all versions carried the same message: *"Give us a treat and we'll bring good luck for the year ahead."* From the chant of *"Up with the kettle and down with the pan"* to lively refrains like *"Ti-ree-raw-raw"* – a descendant of much older mouth music - these songs are as much oral tradition as performance, carried in the memory and mouths of children from generation to generation.

Notably, hospitality and generosity are recurring themes in all these customs. Whether it is welcoming Mary and Joseph through an unbolted door, offering punch to neighbours, or giving coins to wren boys, these acts reflect the value placed on openness, kindness, and shared joy. Even the act of storytelling, whether around the fire or in recalling past Christmases, is an offering. Traditions like lighting three candles for the Trinity, singing Irish-language prayers, or simply coming together in silence, show a cultural reverence for the sacred and the social as inseparable.

This chapter on Traditions also uncovers how Cork people marked the wider season of midwinter, extending from Michaelmas in September to Little Christmas on January 6th. Customs like leaving candles burning for late-night travellers, staying indoors on Christmas Day, or serving women on Epiphany (Women's Christmas), express a yearly cycle of roles and reversals, of sacred observation and local adaptation.

Traditions, by their nature, are both inherited and dynamic. In the testimonies of Cork's older generations, whether it's lighting fires from special "Yule logs" or reciting blessings in Irish, we find customs that continue to evolve. Some traditions remain unchanged, others fade or re-emerge in different forms. Yet in every account, from Tom Healy's memory of the postman's absence to Mrs. Fehin's description of dancing men and disguised boys, one sees how *tradition is never static*. It is a conversation between past and present, always moving, always meaningful.

In exploring these rich customs of Christmas in Cork, this chapter affirms that *traditions are not simply about preserving the old*. They are about expressing values, shaping community, and creating collective meaning. Through ritual, repetition, and celebration, Cork's people have found a way to make the darkest days of the year into the brightest, and to do so together. These traditions, large and small, remind us not only of where we come from, but of who we are.

Christmas in Ireland

The festive season of Christmas is fast approaching. It is a very important festival as the Church gives the permission to give Mass on Christmas at midnight and to fast and abstain during Advent which precedes Christmas. Christmas is looked forward to by young and old, rich and poor. Everyone likes to come home for Christmas if it is at all possible. It is a time of rejoicing, homecomings and reunions. The young children look especially to Christmas more than any other one because Santa Claus fills their Christmas stockings with presents. In Ireland more than any other country there are many customs to be observed. The house is decorated with holly and ivy and different coloured papers. The Christmas candle is lit by a girl named Mary in honour of the Blessed Virgin Mary. In Cork the shopkeepers are very busy during Christmas. The country - folk and the city - folk are very busy doing their Christmas and they buy many provisions for Christmas dinner. Up to this the year the mail was run on Christmas day but this year the postman is exempt. We all miss the postman this Christmas as we cannot get our letters and presents, and we hope that he will enjoy the Christmas as well as ourselves.[29]

Informant: Mr Tom Healy, aged 60, Rathcoola West.

---

[29] The Schools' Collection, Volume 347, p.89.

Christmas Eve

About forty years ago, I spent a good deal of my spare time at my grandfather's home at Shanballyshane at Kilnamartyra. Irish was the main language, rosary always in Irish. The custom invariable on Xmas Eve was: No dinner at usual midday hour. In evening, potatoes and prepared stock fish. Then, before a fire blazing with turf and a special 'scolb', the tea things were brought first, with home-made and purchased Christmas cakes, and afterwards the kettle was put down, when the drinking of "punch" commenced. The Christmas candles had of course been lighted - by the youngest of the house [I do that myself in the town of Macroom still]. This went on, I am afraid up to a late hour, with plenty of songs. Sometimes close neighbours (menfolk) exchanged "calls", but as a rule no strangers were seen that night.[30]

Christmas at Connach

All the houses are whitewashed for Christmas and decorated with holly. On Christmas night all the family are present when the oldest man lights the pound candles that are placed in the windows by the woman of the house. While lighting the candle he blesses himself, genuflects, and then says, "we may all be alive this time twelve months." Then he blesses the house with holy water. Christmas night the people put a big block of wood in the fire and it is called block na Nodlag. Straw is put outside the door Christmas night and the door is let open. The candle in the kitchen is also let lighting and a big fire is put down to comfort Our Lady and the Divine Infant to make up for their hospitality in Bethlehem. Most of the people have two suppers Christmas night potatoes and fish at six o clock and tea at ten o clock. On Christmas day all the people remain in their own houses. On St. Stephen's Day the boys get a holly bush.[31]

Collected in Connach, Co. Cork

---

[30] The Schools' Collection, Volume 0342, p.186.
[31] The Schools' Collection, Volume 306, p.278.

Christmas in Ardgoom

We are back to school again after the Christmas holidays. We had three weeks holidays. It is the greatest feast of the year. It is also the season of great joy in memory of the coming of Jesus Christ. The old people have alot of old customs about Christmas.

They say that all the family should be together at the meals on Christmas eve and on Christmas night. Someone should always stay in the house on Christmas eve. No one should stay out late on Christmas night. We usually have stockfish and gravy made out of butter & new milk for Christmas eve for dinner. We have a turkey or a goose for dinner on Christmas day and Saint Stephen's Day. On St Stephens day the young garsún's comes around to the houses singing the Wren. They used get six pence or a shilling in each house. Then St Stephan's night is a great night by the Wren boys spending the money. The big boys usually go to the dance on that night, but the small boys do not.[32]

Christmas in Riverstick

The old custom of Christmas in this district was, the old people used always have two suppers every Christmas night, they used to have potatoes and fish for the first supper, and they used to have tea after, and Christmas cake, after they had the tea drunk they would sit around the fire then, and have wine and biscuits, and they used to be singing songs also, they would have their homes decorated with holly and ivy, and they used to have tinsil (sic) up on the holly and ivy. They used light the Christmas candle and put it in front of the window, and have it lighting all night. Santa Clause used come Christmas night, and the children used to tie their stockings on to the bed, and there used be toys and sweets in the stockings in the morning. They used to go to six o' clock mass Christmas Morning.

They used to catch the wren Christmas Day for Saint Stephens Day, they used to have a holly-bush and decorate it, and the wren used to be in the centre of the bush.[33]

Collector: Mary Walsh, Riverstick, Co. Cork. Informant: James Walsh.

---

[32] The Schools' Collection, Volume 276, p.444.
[33] The Schools' Collection, Volume 322, p.84.

Christmas in Dromore

It was an ancient Irish Christmas custom to provide a huge stout stump of fir and place it behind the fire on Xmas night. The was called the "Yule Log". It was so large that it used to be kept burning in the fire until the 12th day of Christmas. On Christmas Eve people keep the old custom of eating salt fish or hake and white sauce, and potatoes for the dinner. This meal would not be eaten until four or half past in the evening. Every household is supplied with porter, whiskey, wine no matter how poor they are. And nearly everybody also has an extra supply of food such as all kinds of fruit and other sorts of delicious things too numerous to mention. A roast turkey or goose is nearly everybody's dinner on Xmas Day followed by Plum Pudding. Holly and ivy decorate every house at Christmas. Another local custom is to have a Christmas tree in every house. The tree is decorated with candles, apples, nuts, and other things. The children are delighted with the tree and the presents they get. The Christmas tree is usually taken down on the 6th of January, which is called "Little Christmas".[34]

Collector: Shíle Ní Conchubhair

---

[34] The Schools' Collection, Volume 0294, p.107.

Festival Customs in Derrinagree

On St Stephen's Day boys and men travel round gathering what is called wren money They disguise themselves with high fiddles or coloured faces and wear strange clothes. Sometimes they are dressed as girls or old women. They take with them a staff decorated with holly and ivy and many coloured ribbons or streamers of paper. Sometimes a dead bird supposed to be a wren reposes on this bush. The wren boys go in groups and each group marks out its route beforehand so as to take the pick of the generous houses. They sing wren song and nowadays there is a musician in the group that plays national or popular tunes on a fiddle, pipe, melodeon, or mouth organ. The wren song is:

> The wran the wran the King of all birds
> St. Stephen's Day he was caught in the purge
> Although he is little his family is great
> Cheer up, landlady and give us a "trate"
>
> From bush to bush to tree to tree
> At Derinagree Chapel we broke his knee
> At Drishane castle he had a great fall
> And we brought him here to visit ye all
>
> Up with the kettle and down with the pan
> Give us our answer and let us begone.[35]

Informant: Dan Buckley, Keale North.

---

[35] The Schools' Collection, Volume 0359, p.222.

Figure 10. The Wren Boys. S. C. Hall, Ireland: Its Scenery, Character, vol. 1 (London: How and Parsons, 1841), p.24.

Festival Customs in Meelin

There are certain customs connected with (with) certain feast days. On St. Stephen's Day it is the custom in this part of the country to boys and young men go hunting the Wren. Five or six boys gather together and go off together from house to house with holy bushes in their hands. They dress up very comical, so as not to be known when they would go into a house. They turn their caps and coats inside out and put masks on their faces known as "agaid fiddles."

Some of the party always carry some musical instrument, such as a fiddle, a mouth organ or some other musical instrument. When they go into a house some of the party sing the Wren- Song, others play music and others dance or dance steps. Then the people of the house give them some money of some silver. Then they go off to the next house. The words of the Wren- Song are:

> The Wren, the wren, the king of all birds,
> On St. stephen's Day he was caught in the furze,
> Although he being little, His family [so] is great,
> So cheer up little laddies, and give us a treat,
> Up with the kettle, and down with the pan,
> And give us some money to bury the wren,
> I followed my wren through frost and snow,
> I followed my wren ten miles or more,
> I followed my wren to Killaginish,
> And here I have brought him on a green, holly bush.
> So up with the kettle, and down with the pan,
> And give us some money , to bury the wren.'

The wren boys, as they are called stay out all day until night and gather a good share of money. Some of the Wren boys as they are called divide the money equally among them, some of them keep it for a while and have a good night at some house, while some of them drink it. The "wren boys" that have the dance charge the boys that do not hunt the wren with them, they charge them one shilling or two sometimes.[36]

---

[36] The Schools' Collection, Volume 350, pp.391-392

How We Spend Christmas in Derrycreeveen

Christmas Day is always celebrated on the 25th of December. On the night of Christmas eve everybody lights a Christmas candle in the window of the kitchen and other common candles on the other windows. Everybody hangs strings of holly up on the wall and decoration papers on the loft. Everybody of the family has to be at home before supper time and then the whole family eat supper together. All the children hang their stockings up, near the fire and then everybody goes to bed.

On St Stephen's Day all the boys from about eight years to eighteen go around the parish with a holly bush singing the wren. They have masks and all sorts of coloured papers on them. Every crowd tries to get the wren a couple of days before and hang him on the bush. This is the song they sing:-

> The wren, the wren, the king of all birds,
> St. Stephen's Day he was caught in the furze
> Although he is little,
> His family is great,
> So rise up our landlady,
> And give our boys a treat.
>
> And if the treat be rather small,
> It won't agree with our boys at all,
> But if the treat be, all the best
> I hope in Heaven your soul will rest.
> Chorus
> Ti-ree-raw-raw
> Ti-ree-raw-row
>
> The wren, the wren, that you can see,
> Hanging from our holly tree,
> With a bunch of ribbons by our side,
> And the Bere Island boys to be our guide
> ti-ree-raw-raw,
> ti-ree-raw-raw

> As I went up to Brandy Hall
> I met a wren upon the wall
> Up with my stick and I gave him a fall
> And I brought him here to visit ye all.
> ti-ree-raw-raw,
> ti-ree-raw-raw

When evening comes they all go into some shop and get sweets and lemonade. Then they go home.[37]

Collector: Finbarr Murphy, Derrycreeveen.

Festival Customs in Liscarroll

On St. Stephen's Day, the boys, and grown - up men dress up in queer costumes and go round from house to house collecting money. The boys sing the wren song, which is:

> The wren, the wren, the king of all birds,
> St. Stephen's Day he was caught in the furze.
> Although he was little, his family was great,
> So rise up good landlady and give us a treat.
> We hunted the wren through frost, and snow,
> We hunted this wren ten miles or more
> At Sallypark gate we broke his knee
> And we brought him home on this holly tree
> Mr. O'Brien is a worthy man
> And to his honour we brought this wren
> Bottles of whiskey and bottles of beer
> I wish wou a happy Christmas and New Year.
> Up with the kett;e and down with the pan
> So give us some money to bury the wren.

The boys who go round, and get money buy sweets with their money, or else they keep it, and buy their school's books. Very few boys keep their money because they like enjoying themselves.

The men with their money go to dances, concerts, or entertainments which are held on that night, in the local dance hall. When they went round from house to house, and from place to place they are taken there in motorcars. The people have a good time on that day.

---

[37] The Schools' Collection, Volume 0277, p.23-24.

Christmas Day is the greatest feast day of all, and it lasts twelve days. The people clean up the houses, before they decorate the houses with holly, and ivy. They send Christmas cards to their friends at Christmas. In every house the people have a big dinner on Christmas Day. They cook a goose, or a turkey, and they have plum puddings often.[38]

Collector: Joan Fehin, Liscarroll.
Informant: Mrs Denis Fehin, age 41.

Christmas Customs in Kilcronat

The people around this locality make great preparations for Christmas; they whitewash their houses and decorate them with holly. The heads of the house go to town to do their Christmas shopping. On Christmas Eve, the head of the house lights the Christmas candle and leaves it lighting all night on the window so as to attract the Blessed Virgin to their house; it is believed that the Blessed Virgin wanders around every Christmas Eve as she did in Bethlehem long ago. On Christmas Day, the woman of the house gets up very early and goes up to first mass so as to have the turkey cooked for the dinner and they have plum-pudding after dinner. Christmas night all the family stays at home and they sing songs and play games and tell stories until it is time to go to bed. On St. Stephen's Day, some boys go hunting the wren and they have a holly bush decorated with ribbons and a wren tied on to the bush and they go from house to house singing.

> The Wren the Wren the king of all birds.
> St. Stephen's Day he was caught in the furze.
> Although he was little his family was great.
> Cheer up young lady and give us a treat.

When they have the song sung they usually get money and on St. Stephen's night they have great feasting.[39]

Informant: Mrs. Margaret Casey, aged 55, Kilcronat.

---

[38] The Schools' Collection, Volume 0367, p.186.
[39] The Schools' Collection, Volume 0380, p.273.

Local Customs in Cobh

New Year's Eve Custom. When the clock strikes twelve on New Year's Night the boats that are in the harbour sound their horns. People on the streets beat tin cans. The local band marches through the town playing Old Irish Airs. The Cathedral bells are played by the organist. They send out the old year and they welcome the New Year in. On this same night the old people in some houses in the town beat a piece of bread against the door to keep the hunger out for the coming year as they say.

It is a custom for many years in Cobh to hold a Regatta on the 15th. of August. It is a great day in Cobh. The Regatta is held in the harbour. The boat races begin at three o'clock. There is a bag-race at four o'clock. After that there are balloon races. These races are great fun and the children enjoy them very much. Sixpence is paid for a ticket to send a balloon. A label is tied on to the balloon and the name and address of the person written on it. The balloon that goes the farthest away wins the prize. Whoever finds the balloon sends it back to the address on the label stating where it was picked up. The first prize is a pound.[40]

Informant: Betty Canavan, Cóbh.

---

[40] The Schools' Collection, Volume 0385, pp.527-528.

Figure 11. The Cove of Cobh.

Local Customs in Berrings

It is the custom of the people of this district to light one or two candles on Christmas Eve but in other district people place a candle at every window in the house. Some of the people of this district leave the Christmas Candle lighting all night on Xmas Eve to direct travellers who may be going astray. Some old people in this district say that its right to leave the door unbolted on Christmas Eve to show the Blessed Virgin and Our Lord that there are welcome to their houses.

People who can afford it give many things to the poor during Christmas. On Christmas Eve also almost everybody has some delicacies for their supper and those who can afford it have punch before they go to bed. Some people in this district go to Cork to hear High Mass as Cork City is only about nine miles from Berrings.

Long ago the people used to have their dinner about four or five o'clock in the afternoon on Xmas Eve and then they used to eat their supper about ten o'clock at night. All homes are decorated with holly and ivy and mistletoe and decorations are often used on Xmas Eve. The old people believe that there is an angel in every leaf of holly. The children hang their stockings at the foot of their bed when they are going sleep.

On Christmas Day those who were at confession on Xmas Eve receive Holy Communion and when neighbours meet, they exchange greetings. Hardly anyone goes visiting on Xmas Day as that day is one when the family gather together and talk about the events of the past year. On Xmas Day those who can afford it have a turkey or a goose for their dinner. Those who are away from home try to come home, if possible, for Christmas Day more so than any other time of the year. It is the custom of the youngsters of this district to hunt the wren on Christmas Day. On St. Stephens Day the youngsters of this parish get a holly bush and they decorate it with ribbons. They also put a bit of moss on the bush, and they pretend they have the wren in nest of moss. They go from house to house collecting money and at the same time singing the song?

> The wren, the wren the king of all birds,
> St Stephens Day he was caught in the furze.
> From bush to bush, from tree to tree,
> At Carrigaline he broke his knee.
> Up with the kettle and down with the pot,
> Give us our answer and let us be off.

When evening comes, they buy food with the money which they collected.

On New Year's Eve many people remain up until midnight to bring in the new year. Candles are also light on this night. On New Year's Day people wish each other a happy and a prosperous new year. The 6th of January is often called Little Christmas or the Women's Christmas. Some people say the reason why this day is called the Women's Xmas is because the women are supposed to be served by the men as the women have served the men during the beginning of Xmas.

It was the custom of the young people long ago, to gather old buckets and old tin cans and tie them together with a string on Shrove Tuesday. Then they used to go to the houses of those whom they thought should be married. They used to say that they were hunting them to Skellig Rock in Kerry. Then the young people used to make songs about the old people and these songs we called Skellig Lists.

Shrove Tuesday is often called Pancake Night because long ago it was the custom to have a little feast of pan cakes as Shrove Tuesday is the Tuesday before Ash-Wednesday. Pan cakes were made with flour, milk and eggs and were cooked in a pan.[41]

Collector: Con O'Herlihy, Berrings.

---

[41] The Schools' Collection, Volume 0348, pp.94-98.

Christmas Customs in Ballyhea

There are a lot of customs connected with Christmas in Ballyhea such as cleaning the house and decorating it with holly and ivy and buying a turkey for the Christmas dinner and getting wine and lemonade and whiskey and stout. On Christmas day there are four masses said and it is dark when the people are going to mass and when they come home they have a piece of ham for their breakfast. Then they are very busy preparing the turkey for the dinner and when the people come home from second mass they sit around the table and eat their dinner and after the dinner they have a plum pudding. Everyone stays at home that day When night comes there is a big block put in the fire and three candles are lighted in honour of the Father, Son, and Holy Ghost. Then the table is put in the middle of the floor and the supper is got. Then the wine and lemonade is given out and some one of the family sings a song or tells a story.

On St Stephens day all the small boys go out hunting the wren and they put on the worst clothes they in order that the people would not know them and when they come near a house the say.

> The wren the wren
> The king of all birds
> St Stephen's day he was caugh in the furze.
> Up with the kettle and down with the pot.
> Give us our answer and let us be off.

Then the people give them something and they go away. Nearly all the men got hunting on that day. The children look forward to Christmas because they hang up their stockings for Santa Claus to give them presents.[42]

Collector: Julia O' Keeffe, Castlewrixon

---

[42] The Schools' Collection, Volume 374, pp.363-365.

Local Customs in Conna

In ancient years, the people of Ireland were much more Irish than those of the present day. The old Irish people, as we have read in our history lessons, were very fond of old customs. On some nights of the year, they had special customs, but as time flies, these customs are rapidly fading away.

New Year's night was one of the nights on which the people had a special custom. On that night, the people used to go to the house of the oldest person in the district. They would knock at the door and when the person would come to the door, they would say: "A hundred thousand welcomes to you, a hundred thousand welcomes to you, a hundred thousand welcomes to you, the chief of the house." The person would then invite them in and give them a drink. This was called "Céad Míle Fáilte". It was a very old custom and is not observed now.

Another custom was the First Foot. The first person to enter a house on New Year's Day was supposed to bring luck to the house for the year. If a tall, dark man entered, it was considered very lucky. If a woman or a light-haired man entered, it was considered unlucky.

On St. Stephen's Day, the boys used to go around the district hunting the wren. They would dress up in old clothes and go from house to house singing:

> The wren, the wren, the king of all birds,
> St. Stephen's Day was caught in the furze.
> Although he is little, his family is great,
> Jump up, me lads, and give us a treat.

They would then collect money and sometimes a drink. This was called "Hunting the Wren".

These are some of the old customs that were observed in Ireland in former times.[43]

Collected at Conna.

---

[43] The Schools' Collection, Volume 0380, p.70.

The Wren Boys in Glan

With the approach of Christmas and Saint Stephen's Day the boys of the land begin to think of the wren. They go from house to house singing the wren song. On Christmas Day they hunt up the wren trying to catch and kill a little bird. If they fail to find a wren-hoping to kill it with sticks and stones, which they seldom do-- they get a lump of moss and put it in a holly branch saying that a wren is in the nest formed of moss. They get a stick and tie a branch of holly on top of it in which is supposed to be the wren. They decorate it with ribbon and strips of coloured paper.

On Saint Stephen's Day morning they meet at some place appointed and dress up with ribbons, and hats of coloured paper. One is a clown, and he blackened his face and hands, with either soot or black boot polish. One carries the holly bush. When dressed they sally forth. They make a gay sight - coloured ribbons and paper floating in the breeze. The clown with his black face and dressed in brilliant colours acts half-foolishly as it were. They must also provide a moneybox. If a right one is not in their possession the get a tin box - usually a cocoa-box - and cut a slit in the cover, having already bound on the cover. They let the money drop in the slit. One of them also carries a bugle or horn. I've seen a large kind of a seashell use as a bugle, which they sounded meaning every house to tell they were coming. A bottle is also used.

They sing the wren song at every house, and they get money from the man of the house. At some houses they get tea. After the day's travelling, they divide the money among themselves, or sometimes they use it on food and other things which they take to some house and hold a dance there. By singing the wren song they earn the money. The following is the song which is sung:

I
The wran, the wran, the king of all birds,
St. Stephen's Day, he was caught in the furze.
Although he is little his family is great.
Rise up landlady and give us a trate

II

And if you fill it of the best,
In heaven I hope your soul will rest:
But if you fill it of the small,
It won't agree with our boys at all.

III

Christmas night and I turning the spit
I burned my finger, I feel it yet -
Between my finger and my thumb,
There lies a blister as big as a plum

IV

Sing holly, sing ivy, sing ivy, sing holly,
Christmas times are all very jolly,
Christmas comes but once a year,
And when it comes it brings good cheer.

V

And you Mr. O. being a worthy man,.
'Tis to your house we brought our wran;
We brought our "wran" for to visit you here.
Not for a taste of your liquor or a drink of your beer,
But to wish you a merry Christmas and a Happy New Year.
With your pockets full of money and your cellars full of beer.

VI

Here is our wran you may plainly see,
He is mounted high on a holly tree,
With a bunch of ribbons by his side;
And the Glaun boys to be his guide,
So up with the kettle and down with the pan,
Give us our answer and let us be gone.[44]

Collected at Glan.

---

[44] The Schools' Collection, Volume 1128, pp.20-23.

I think of thee Dear Drimoleague

This is another fine old song which I took down from Con O'Mahony, Droumousta, during the summer of 1936. He informed me this song seen in print and he related to me as follows, how and by whom it was composed. Those are his words.

About forty years ago there lived in the village of Drimoleague a family named Coakley. The family consisted of two boys Jack and Dan and a girl named Ellie. They all received a good sound education in the old school in Drimoleague and after spending a few years working around the village Jack, together with a cousin of his one Houlihan of Lehana joined the British Navy.

The Houlihans were a gifted family and were great poets. However, one Christmas when Jack Coakley and his cousin Houlihan were in foreign service in Madras Bay, and miles and miles from their old native homes, they got their heads together, and composed the following song about Drimoleague

I
I think of thee Dear Drimoleague on High Stret there's my home
From Brother dear and sister kind from them I had to roam
To a foreign land neath alien skies and over there am I
But wherein I roam sure I'm proud to own I'm a proud
young Drimoleague Boy

II
When I think of my own school mates, they are now all grown up men
And of my childhood happy days I wish them back again
When my young heart no trouble knew, nor danger did i see
O'er the ocean's track my thoughts fly back Sweet Drimoleague to thee

III
Tis well I do remember the Drimoleague quarries old
And the gallant men who worked in them with courage stout and bold.
Their names are famed in History for their workmanship and skill
They like brothers helped each other at the crowbar and the drill

IV
And God be with you Meenie's groves where oft times I have been
When I rambled through the wild wood then to pluck the Holly Green
And to O'Donovan's Castle my thoughts would fondly stray
Where I used to roam with my sweetheart on many a Christmas Day

V

From my father's home in High Street Owen mountains can be seen
Where the river Ilen rises and flows into Skibbereen
There grows the heather green and wild and many a Poteen Still
Well hidden in the bosom of Owen's lofty Hill

VI

Dan Coakley is my father's name I'm proud to own and tell.
T'was tenderly he reared me as the neighbours all can tell.
In many a field he laboured from the village to Drimoleague
While I was young and happy there at home in Drimoleague.

Explanatory notes

High Street: A lofty eminence overlooking the village the scene of many a faction fight in the olden days

Meenies: A townland two and a half miles North West of Drimoleague, the scene of a one-time beautiful wood, now practically cut down. It was a custom with the lads of the village to travel to Meenies a few days before Xmas to pluck the Holly Green.

Castle Donovan: The ancient seat of the O'Donovan clan The Castle can still be seen. A comthalán or "pattern" was held there on Christmas Day in olden times

Owen Hill: Cnoc na n-abhann so called because three rivers The Ilen (An Aidhle), the Mealagh (An Mhealach) and the Bandon (An Bhandan) have their source there in a bunch of luachair. Many an Irish still flourishes among the Heather where the best of Irish Poteen can be had for the asking.

Doirín na Spéig: a townland situated 3 miles east of Drimoleague[45]

Informant: Con O' Mahony, Dromasta.

---

[45] The Schools' Collection, Volume 0299, pp.217-221.

One Christmas Eve in Dublin

Come buy my nice fresh ivy and my holly sprigs so green;
I have the finest branches that ever yet were seen.
Come buy from me, good Christians, and let me home I pray;
And I'll wish you Merry Christmas times and a happy New Year's Day.

Ah! Won't you take my ivy the loveliest ever seen
Ah! won't you have my holly boughs all you who love the green,
Do take a little bunch of each on my knees I'll pray
That God may bless your Christmas and your New Year's Day.

I have the finest holly and the finest ivy too
I have the finest branches that ever yet were grew.
Come buy from me, good Christians, and let me home I pray
And I'll wish you Merry Christmas and a happy New Year's Day.

I have the finest holly and the finest ivy too
I have the finest branches that ever yet were grew.
Come buy from me, good Christians, and let me home I pray
And I'll wish you Merry Christmas and a happy New Year's Day.[46]

Informant: Charles Mac Carthy, aged c. 65. Ballydehob.

---

[46] The Schools' Collection, Volume 0290, p.383.

The Sthickeen

The highest point of Carrigfadtha hill - a few miles due south of Drinagh is called the Sticín. From this hill a great view is obtained of the southern seaboard, from Roaring water to Bantry Clonakilty Bay. People from all parts assemble here on Christmas day and indulge in stone throwing and leaping. It seems strange that this day should be selected for such a cold exposed place at this time of year with poor visibility. Some old residents think that the custom has come down from Penal days when Mass on the Mountain was celebrated and of course Christmas Day would attract an immense number of people to the spot at such a time. If not disturbed by military there would be a tendency to diversion after Mass and the usual games of strength and skill would be indulged in between the champions of the different parishes.[47]

The Harvest of the Geese

The Harvest of the Geese is the period in the fall of the year when the young tender geese are being killed. The first goose of the season is eaten on Michaelmas Day September 29th and the geese are killed and eaten at the rate of about one each week usually for Sunday's dinner. While the young geese last is generally referred to as the "Harvest of the Geese". Thus, the season usually extends from Michaelmas until Christmas.

The geese are plucked twice a year. The first plucking is done in July and the second plucking is in September or October (early Oct.)

The geese lay for the Well-day that is on the feast of St Burceart who had his church in Tullylease Co Cork a distance of five miles from Meelin. A goose lays about fifteen eggs in all and at the rate of about five each week. Shortly after stopping laying the goose begins to hatch and then from about a dozen to fifteen eggs are put under her. It takes her four weeks to hatch the same time as it takes for duck-eggs. The eggs of the goose are kept in bran to protect them from the air until the goose hatches.[48]

Informant: Mrs John P Browne, Knockeen, Meelin, Newmarket.

---

[47] The Schools' Collection, Volume 0303, p.436.
[48] The Schools' Collection, Volume 0350, p.134.

Hunting the Wren in Lombardstown

In this district (Glantane, Lombardstown, Co. Cork) about fifty years ago the boys used to come together on Christmas Day after dinner and go hunting the wren. Each boy was provided with a stick or had a stone in each hand ready to throw it at the poor little bird when routed out of its hiding place.

    The boys divided into two companies, one going along at each side of a hedge or fence of furze bushes. One or two of the boys in front at each side were told off as "beaters"; their duty being to strike each bush with the sticks as they went along and they generally accompanied the strokes with the cry "Hi, Dreoilín!"

    When a wren was seen the shout "Here she is" was raised; each boy tried to knock the little bird with stick or stone. Everyone carefully noted the next resting place if the wren escaped the first volley, and so the pursuit was carried on until an dreoilín was killed or succeeded in concealing itself in a loose stone fence or a very thick hedge where it could not be found. If they failed to kill the first one met, they continued the hunt until they succeeded, if if possible, because at that time the boys would not go from house to house without having a wren tied on the holly bush which was carried by the leader of the procession on St. Stephen's Day.

    Occasionally the reason given by a person for refusing to contribute was that it was cruelty to kill the "poor innocent little wren". But if the dead wren was not to be seen others gave its absence as an excuse for not giving any contribution.[49]

Collector: T. Coleman.

---

[49] The Schools' Collection, Volume 0362, pp.194-195.

The Local Fairs

The local farmers are very well situated as regards the fair. There is a fair held at Mallow the first Tuesday in the month and there is a fair held at Coachford the second Tuesday in the month and there is a fair held at the Half-way house on the first Friday of the month and there is a fair held at New Tipperary every third Tuesday in the month. There is a special fair field for each fair. There are special fairs held at Mallow on the 30th of October, New Year's Day and the 5th of August. There is a horse show held in Dublin every year and crowds of people come from all parts of Ireland to see it. There is a special fair field for the fair in New Tipperary and the jobbers come there every third Tuesday in the month. There is a special fair for horses and a special fair held for sheep, cattle, and pigs. After every purchase a coin is returned to the buyer for "luck". The buyers come come round to the houses to buy pigs and the pigs are taken to the slaughterhouse in Cork or Limerick.[50]

Informant: Mr J. O'Hanlon, aged 57, Farmer, Ahadallane.

---

[50] The Schools' Collection, Volume 0347, p.87.

The Runaway Bog
A Song from Rathmore

I
Upon that wild December night poor Donnelly went to rest
With his loving wife and children by the heaven he was blest.
The joys of Christmas singing around his humble cot.
But are the morning it had come it proved a treacherous spot.

II
Whilst those people sound were sleeping in the quiet it is supposed.
Down from the hills all around the floods and torrents roared.
And carried all before it their lives and property.
Their homes were swept all were plunged into eternity.

III
Next morning what an awful sight
the neighbours did behold,
A countryside of misery was covered
with turf and mold
They organised the party for miles to
search around
For the bodies of the victims they tried every inch of ground

IV
Before it reached Headford some
bridge was thrown down
And people cried loudly "Tis making for the town.
It was the will of Providence that broke this bogaway
And emptied in Killarney lakes
Thank God I'm glad to say.

Supposed to be composed by Joe Dineen who was a brother to An tAthair Pádruig (of Dictionary fame) - Joe died 23/6/1928.[51]

Collector: Hugh Mc Carthy, Knocknagree.
Informant: David Murphy, aged 84.

---

[51] The Schools' Collection, Volume 0357, pp.307-308.

Winter Games - Outdoor - Boys and Girls

Judy and Jack. - Two children stand behind each other with hands caught. They go along on tip toe skipping lively, and repeating.

> Judy and Jack, dressed in black,
> Silvery buttons behind their backs.
> * Hey, hó, tippedy toe
> Turn the ship, and away we go.
> They then do right about turn, and repeat the game.
> (This is an outdoor game for a cold, frosty, dry day)
> * Sometimes - "Tiny tip and tiny toe
> Turn the ship and away we go."

Burn the Biscuit - A biscuit, a sweet, or some other small article is hidden by one player in the kitchen. All the others search for it. Whoever finds it has permission to eat it, and hide something else.

Horny, horny Cow's horn - Four players sit near the fire. A handkerchief is stretched between them, each player holding a corner with his left hand. The first finger of the right hand is stretched forward, and placed on the handkerchief. For each horned-animal named, the finger is raised on high. If raised in mistake, that player gets a slap, or has to pay a forfeit. The leader then begins, moving his finger swiftly on the handkerchief, and repeating as quickly as possible.

> Horny, Horny! Horny, Horny! Horny, Horny! Cow's horn

or perhaps

> Horny, horny! Horny-horny! Horny-horny - Cat's horn.

The leader sometimes tries to mislead the players, by raising his finger for the horn less animals, or vice versa.

Collector: John Barry, Banteer.
Informant: Michael Sheehan, Inchidaly.

Reflections

As we close this chapter, what emerges most clearly is that traditions are not merely the leftovers of history. In County Cork, a land of strong memory and strong community, traditions are living things. They are acts of remembrance, of cultural creativity, and of belonging. They are performed in kitchens and country lanes, told in story and song, passed from child to child, elder to youth, and they are renewed each year with both reverence and joy.

This is nowhere more evident than in the vivid, often deeply personal, accounts of Christmas that have been passed down, preserved, and shared by generations of Cork people. These are not abstract or academic observations. They are warm fireside recollections, worn with time, softened by memory, and sharpened by detail. They show us the texture of rural life, a life in which tradition was not something optional or ceremonial, but essential.

In every village and townland, from Ballyhea to Riverstick, from Knocknagree to Glantane, Christmas in Cork was (and still is) a time of sacred rhythm and rootedness. It follows its own pattern, shaped by the season and liturgical calendar, but also by family dynamics, local lore, and Irish identity. Even the most modest household prepared for Christmas with a sense of purpose: whitewashing the walls, gathering holly, lighting candles, preparing simple or splendid meals. These actions may seem ordinary on the surface, but within them lie centuries of layered meaning.

We see, in these customs, a powerful expression of faith, not only Catholic in form, but also spiritual in its embrace of hospitality, light, and hope. The practice of lighting a candle on Christmas Eve "so that Mary and Joseph might find their way" transforms a humble window into a portal of welcome. The act of keeping the door unbolted, placing straw at the threshold, or setting aside the best firewood for the Christ child speaks not only to religious belief, but to an ethic of generosity that cuts across class, region, and age.

Just as clearly, these traditions demonstrate how folklore and faith are intertwined. The wren boys, disguised in tattered clothes and masked with soot, may appear to be a purely secular spectacle, a day of mischief and music. But they echo ancient sacrificial rites, midwinter fertility customs, and even resistance to colonial suppression of native Irish festivals. Singing the Wren Song becomes not just entertainment, but a performance of identity. In dressing up, collecting coins, and invoking local place names, Kilaginish, Carrigaline, Brandy Hall, the boys perform a ritual of belonging, linking their local world to a mythic past.

These customs also show that tradition is communal before it is individual. Christmas, as described in nearly every account, is about being home, not just physically, but emotionally and spiritually. The family must be together on Christmas Eve. No one is to stay out late. Two suppers must be had. Songs must be sung. Candles must be lit. Stories must be told. These are not optional extras but essential rituals, reinforcing the message that everyone has a place at the hearth, and that the passing of time is best marked through shared experience.

Even the smallest details in these traditions carry cultural weight. The stockfish and white sauce of Christmas Eve is more than a meal, it is a signal of sacred anticipation, of fasting before feasting. The plum pudding, the Christmas punch, the turkey or goose, the candles in the windows, these repeat across accounts like seasonal incantations, anchoring the present in the past. Likewise, the song lyrics, reappearing in slightly different forms in every parish, form a kind of oral map of Cork's Christmas, echoing through Keale North, Bere Island, Ballydehob, and Dromasta with joyous familiarity.

But perhaps most striking of all is how these traditions balance reverence and revelry, sacredness, and celebration. The quiet lighting of the Trinity candles and blessing of the home coexists with boys playing bugles and dancing in painted coats. The solemn attendance at midnight Mass is followed by storytelling, music, and even mischief. This harmony is at the heart of Cork's traditions, a culture where ritual and fun are not opposites, but complements.

There is also a powerful sense of cyclical time in these traditions. The year, as remembered in these narratives, is not a flat sequence of months, but a wheel turning through festival and fast, feast and reflection. Christmas begins weeks before with Advent preparation, then extends through New Year's Eve customs, to Little Christmas (January 6th), and in some accounts, even further, to Shrove Tuesday's Pancake Night, Michaelmas goose dinners, and the Harvest of the Geese. Every feast day and seasonal marker becomes a thread in a rich tapestry of communal timekeeping, one that is spiritual, agrarian, and local.

As much as these accounts preserve memory, they also reveal change and adaptation. Traditions shift: the real wren becomes a mossy decoy, the stockfish gives way to more modern meals, the fiddle is replaced by a mouth organ, and now perhaps by a speaker and smartphone. But the essence remains: a community performing its story, year after year. Change does not erase tradition; it reshapes it, proving it is alive.

This chapter has offered more than a glimpse into festive customs. It has opened a window into a worldview, a way of life where home, place, memory, and the sacred are interwoven. In every candle lit, every song sung, every treat given to the wren boys, Cork people affirm something profound: that tradition is a way of saying "we are still here." It is a way of thanking those who came before, welcoming those who are present, and making space for those yet to come.

In an age of speed and disconnection, these traditions offer something increasingly rare: a rhythm of slowness, rootedness, and shared meaning. They remind us that celebration does not need extravagance; it needs sincerity. That faith is not confined to church walls, it lives in the light of a window candle. That family is not just blood, it is the shared stories, songs, and food that gather us around the fire.

So, whether it is the soft prayer before lighting the candle, the laughter of boys dressed in ribbons, or the hum of an old wren song drifting down a country road, the traditions of Cork remind us that culture is not something we inherit passively, it is something we practice, year after year, together. And in practicing it, we do not just remember the past, we shape the future.

6

Winter Weather

Winter in rural Ireland is more than just a season; it is a time of reckoning, a test of endurance, and a wellspring of memory. In this chapter we turn to the deep and enduring relationship between Cork's people and the coldest, darkest time of year. Through the local recollections of storms, snowfalls, and survival, we come to understand winter not just as climate, but as a cultural force shaping the land, the people, and their traditions.

In these stories, drawn from places like Ballydehob, Dunbeacon, Ballinglanna, and Boherboy, winter is remembered not in mild inconveniences or romantic imagery, but as a season of profound disruption. Roads were blocked, houses buried, animals lost, and trains halted. People speak of waking to find their doors blocked by snowdrifts higher than the roof, of children not christened for six weeks because no path could be cut to the chapel, of animals dug from frozen ground by the warmth of their own breath.

The memories begin with storms, some of them legendary. The Great Storm of 1839, known as Oíche na Gaoithe Móire (Night of the Big Wind), left a mark not just on the landscape but on the folklore of the people. It was said that three children were born that night, and none would die until they performed miracles. The storm itself tore apart houses, blew hay into rivers, and claimed the lives of young children drowned when bridges were blocked and burst by rising water. These were not simply acts of nature; they were seen as events filled with divine warning or mystery.

In 1926 and again in 1927, great floods and storms swept Cork. People recalled rivers flooding homes, cattle swept away, boats wrecked, and roofs stripped bare by wind. Trains were halted by fallen trees; entire districts became isolated. The storm of 1928 was so devastating it "knocked down nearly all the trees in the country," blocking roads and cutting families off from Christmas gatherings. It was not uncommon to read phrases like "many people could not come home for Christmas." The physical storm became a metaphor for separation, loneliness, and the fragility of daily life.

But it was not just storms. It was snow, deep and deadly, that seemed to capture most powerfully the essence of Irish winters in local memory. The snow of 1902, said to be fifteen feet deep in sheltered areas, rendered Cork's countryside impassable. It entered houses through keyholes and roof slates. Water wells froze; paths had to be dug to find livestock; people melted snow for drinking water, which boiled 'as black as soot.' The fragility of infrastructure and the resilience of people stood in sharp contrast. One account noted that people who couldn't access the well would boil snow and drink it, blackened with soot and impurities, because there was no alternative.

Perhaps the most storied snowfall was The Big Snow, variously dated to 1853, 1854, 1856, or 1893, depending on the region. These events became markers of time. Babies born during these winters were remembered as "born the year of the big snow." In Enniskean, the snow came so suddenly that it covered entire homes overnight. In Ballinglanna, women rowed boats for provisions across frozen inlets. In Boherboy, snow entered houses through window frames and piled up inside. The wind was so fierce it blew through every gap in the timber, and without well-insulated homes, families relied on luck, prayer, and heavy clothing for survival.

Animals feature centrally in these winter memories. Farmers recall finding sheep buried but still alive, their breath melting hollows in the drifts. Goats were rescued after days trapped under snowbanks; their calls muffled until a small breathing hole revealed their hiding place. These stories are not just quaint, they reflect a deep connection between humans and animals in rural life, and how winter hardship was shared across species.

The hardships were severe, but so too was the response of the community. Neighbours dug paths not just for themselves but for others. Stories describe men cutting through miles of snow to reopen roads, rescuing livestock, or retrieving priests unable to say Mass. When storm or snow hit, community life paused, but also pulled together. Beggars were taken in, goats rescued, and fires shared. In some places, the drifts remained visible until May, a reminder of how long-lasting a single winter event could be.

And yet, through all this, the Irish people, especially in Cork, found ways to record and retell. Winter was not just endured, it was woven into oral tradition, into songs, ballads, and fireside stories. The storm became legend, the snow a local chapter in a community's collective memory. Every house had a tale: of the priest who couldn't reach the altar, the sheep buried but alive, the train that never arrived, or the child born during a blizzard who lived to a hundred.

In a place like Ireland, where the calendar year was once closely tied to the agricultural and liturgical seasons, winter marked a necessary time of stillness and story. The land rested. So did the people. And in that resting, they remembered. These stories became their inheritance, and this chapter seeks to preserve that inheritance.

In modern Ireland, snowploughs and electric heaters may have softened the edges of winter's bite, but the stories remain. They are reminders of a time when weather was not just news, but a force of nature, shaping lives, testing strength, and forming legends.

As we begin this chapter on Winter, we do so not only to recall hardship, but to honour the resilience, ingenuity, and humanity of those who faced it. In Cork's fields and valleys, in its stone cottages and coastal villages, winter brought silence and storm, but also kinship, memory, and enduring tradition. This is a season not just of cold, but of character.

Severe Weather in Ballydebob

On Christmas Night 1927 there was a great storm. Rivers rose and flooded fields, and drowned cattle and sheep. The flood went into houses in the low ground and flooded them. Trees were knocked by the wind, and it caused many accidents. Boats were wrecked. Roofs were stripped of their slate. Houses were knocked. Trees were knocked across the rails of the railroad tracks causing the trains to stop till were removed.[52]

Collector: Michael O'Regan, Ballydehob.

Snow at Ballydehob

The greatest snow that was ever seen around here within living memory was in the year 1902. It was about fifteen feet high in low level sheltery places and about four feet high in the rocky places. It was so high up that it used go in the key holes of the doors.

There was a heavy gale blowing with it that used almost drive it in through the slates of the houses. The people could not go outside the doors to do anything without getting shovels and spades and other things to clear away paths to walk.

The people could not get any water. They should also make paths to the wells. When they used reach the wells they used be frozen and covered up with sleet and snow. Then they should get snow and put it in the kettle instead of water. When it was boiled it was as black as soot

When they used go looking for their sheep they used find them after a long search lying down near the ditches and their breath used keep away the snow. The snow lasted eight days in the low places.[53]

Collector: Kitty Kennedy, Ballybane West

---

[52] The Schools' Collection, Volume 0291, p.70.
[53] The Schools' Collection, Volume 0289, pp.22-23.

Local Happenings

There was a great storm in the year 1839 on little Christmas night. Three people were born on that night and it was believed by the people that they would not leave without doing some miracle.

There was a great flood in the year 1926. There were three children of Michael Fitzgerald of Lower Road drowned.

There was a field of hay near Allen's Bridge and the wines of hay were blown into the river, and they blocked the eye of the bridge. The water rushed out and flowed into the house and drowned the three children.

In 1928 there was a great storm. It knocked down nearly all the trees in the country. There was a bus going from Newmarket to Cork and it was blocked in the road by trees and had to go around by Liscarrol. Many people could not come home for Christmas because all the roads were blocked with trees.[54]

Collector: Phillip O'Reardan, Newmarket.

---

[54] The Schools' Collection, Volume 0353, Page 236

A Snowstorm at Dunbeacon

About eighty years ago a great snowstorm which lasted over a week caused much destruction. The snow rose higher than the houses, so that for a few days nobody ventured out. Everything was in a pitiable condition. The people could not get water, fuel, or any eatables so that when the snow melted, the people were almost dying from cold and hunger. The animals also suffered immensely. They could not be attended to, and my grandfather said that about twenty animals died in our townland.

Great was the number of birds which perished, on the roads, and fields. An island south of Carbery Island in Dunmanus Bay, called Bird Island is said to derive its name from the numerous amount of birds which were found dead on it after this snowstorm.[55]

Collector: Mary J. Moynihan, Drishane, Co. Cork
Informant: Richard Moynihan, aged 58.

Snowfall in Derreennalomane

About the year 1892 there came a great snow in this part of the county. The snow was so great that it came in through the slate in some houses and in through the keyholes in the doors. The outhouses were filled with snow in the morning and the people had a great difficulty in finding their cattle. There were no lives lost in this locality but there were a lot of sheep lost on the hills.

The snow was about three feet high in the ground, and in some place it rose to ten feet because the snow was dry and light and the storm drifted it along. It was on a Sunday morning and the priests had great difficulty in travelling. Father Bernard was in Ballydehob at the time and he was going to say mass in Dunbeacon and he was unable to go beyond Dreenlomane School cross. The snow lasted for about a week on the ground and the birds all died with the hunger.[56]

Collector: Alice Hayes, Derreennalomane.
Informant: Mr John Driscoll, aged 74, Letter.

---

[55] The Schools' Collection, Volume 0289, p.133.
[56] The Schools' Collection, Volume 0293, pp.47-48.

Big Snow in Enniskean - November 1854

This was a huge snowfall, and we got a description of it from a very old woman, Mrs. Hallahan, aged 90. She says the days before were very fine and snow was not expected but during the night it fell so thickly that it covered the houses completely in one night. When the people arose in the morning, they were greatly surprised to see that they could not go outside their doors, the snow had all places so blocked up. All animals out in the fields were covered, and men were engaged in digging the snow from one town to the other, to make a passage to let the traffic pass. Other men were engaged in digging paths from their doors in order to make passages through which they could travel. To make matters worse there was a hard frost during the night and that hardened the snow with the result of making tasks much harder for the men who were making the passages. People had to melt the snow for water as they could not go to the well to obtain it. In that year the farmers suffered much because their stock were suffocated in the snow, the few animals that were alive were discovered by their breathing.[57]

Collector: Séamus Ó Lordáin, Enniskean.
Informant: Mrs. Hallahan, aged 91, Ardkitt West.

Snowstorm in Derryduff about 50 years

A workman told the following tale of woe. He lived at Derryduff and was a workman to Stephen Fitzpatrick. One night his wife fell ill, and he sped in haste for a local nurse, Mrs Harold, he brought her along in a pannier until she fell through it and he arrived home with the nurse in good time to find his wife had given birth to twin girls.

Snowstorm of 1856 came on a Shrove Tuesday. It lasted three weeks. It was as high as the houses. People had to make passages to the well etc. The snow was so firm and hard that people could walk on top of it and the beggars stayed for three weeks in houses.[58]

---

[57] The Schools' Collection, Volume 0306, p.219.
[58] The Schools' Collection, Volume 0316, Page 096

The Year of the Big Snow - Ballinglanna in 1853

There is a man in Ballinglanna that was born the year of the big snow. They couldn't take the baby to the chapel to be christened for 6 weeks. The people around the seaside used to take boats to the town for their provisions. The women at that time used to do the oaring as well as the men.[59]

Informant: Bat Donovan, aged 60, worker and fisherman, Ballinglanna.

A Great Snowstorm in Boherboy

A great snowstorm occurred in this district in the end of February, and, as far as I can make out, it was in the year 1893.

Prior to the storm the weather was intensely cold, with a strong wind blowing from the east. The sky was dark and gloomy, and birds and animals sought shelter wherever they could find it before the approach of the storm.

It began about three o'clock in the afternoon. The flakes were very small and hard and blown with great force. Nobody could go out into the open for fear of getting smothered. The flakes were so small that they entered the house through keyholes, between doors and frames of doors, even in between the window frames. I need hardly say that the houses were not as air-tight then as they are now. Most of the houses were in poor repair. The doors were often broken and the windows without panes.

At all events the snow was blown into the houses and was lying in heaps inside the doors and windows. Both people and animals had to remain where they were when the storm began. It raged all through the night with increasing fury and showed no signs of abating till the approach of morning when it gradually eased off. But when day arrived there was no sign of its appearance indoors, because the snow inside the doors and windows (where the houses were not in good repair) was as high as the walls and outside it was as high as the houses.

The drifts were in some places 10 or 12 feet high. The first thing to be done was to try to dig a passage out through the door - a difficult feat when it is borne in mind that the snow outside was as high as the house. I remember the day well because as I was then very young (about 10 years) and as it was impossible to go out I was forced to remain in bed most of the day. It was impossible to reach out-houses so that the cattle in

---

[59] The Schools' Collection, Volume 0318, p.39.

them had to go without either food or water for that day, while sheep and other animals out-of-doors were mostly smothered.

The people were in many cases in a bad plight also. Unless they had turf and water inside since the previous day they had to do without both, If they were lucky enough to have turf inside they were able to make a fire and so they could melt some snow, to make water. If they had no turf inside they had to go without fire and had to subsist on any morsels of food left since the previous day. [At that time bread was rarely found in the houses of the poor, or even in the houses of most farmers. They subsisted on potatoes, which they used three times a day with sour milk and a pinch of salt, as long as they had them. At other times they made "gruel" from Indian meal or they used oaten meal raw (they put a handful of it into a basin of milk (sweet, sour, or thick) and ate the mixture]

Those who had no bread on this day and who were without a store of potatoes in the house had to remain without food. Towards evening a thaw set in and it began to rain heavily. The thaw and rain continued all night, and when next morning arrived only the drifts remained, and these were still very deep, so that passages had to be cut through them for cattle to be driven to get water. Sheep perished by the thousand everywhere, although some of them were later found alive under the drifts. This is the worst snowstorm I can remember.

Here is a little story in connection with it and a true one: At that time people kept goats in much greater numbers than we do now. We had three or four. Goats' milk was in great favour for colouring tea and even for drinking purposes. I remember well that one of the goats was missing for days, and of course we were under the impression that it was dead in a drift. Well, about 6 days after the blizzard I was standing near a drift not far from our house. I heard an animal bleating not far away. I looked around but could see nothing. Still the bleating continued. I continued to examine my surroundings but could not see nothing, and I was beginning to think that the place was haunted. After a while I climbed up on the drift. I noticed a hole coming up right through it from the ground - a very tiny hole and the snow surrounding it discoloured, as it is when thawing. I thought this very strange, and I was wondering what caused it when I again heard the "Baa! Baa!" I tried to locate the sound again. After a while it dawned on me that it was coming through the hole in the snow. I ran in home to tell my father, but at first he only ridiculed me. However, I persuaded him to come out. He cleared the drift in the direction of the hole and there inside was the goat nice and cosy. The snow had protected it from the cold, while it was able to breathe through the hole; and if it required water it had only to chew the snow. The above story is true in every detail. I forgot to mention that this drift was near a steep bank against which the goat was sheltering when overtaken by the blizzard. So huge were the drifts that they were still to be seen in sheltered places in the month of May. Children, who delight to go barefooted in country places, used to enjoy themselves playing pranks. At the edge of a drift and then running out into the clear ground where the sun was shining brightly to warm their feet.[60]

       Collector: John Galvin, teacher, Islandbrack.

A Snowstorm in Fermoy

I have heard locally that eighty-two and ninety years ago a great snowstorm occurred around this locality. It was from forty to fifty feet high, which was covering some of the houses and nearly level with others, so that any person looking from some height he would only see the snow, covering all the ground, just the same as a white carpet, no ditches or hedges or anything at all to be seen. All traffic on the roads and also on the railway line was stopped on account of the snow blocking the roads and also blocking the railway line. The people also were unable to get out of their houses on account of the snow blocking the doorway. After the snow falling on the ground, it froze, which made it a lot harder for people to make their way through the snow. Animals and birds too, were in a wretched condition, because they could not get food or drink on account of the snow and frost on the ground. Children were unable to go to school on account of this great snowstorm, which lasted for a couple of months.[61]

   Collector: Con Fitzgerald, Fermoy., Informant: Mr M. Fitzgerald, aged 50.

---

[60] The Schools' Collection, Volume 0355, p.120-124.
[61] The Schools' Collection, Volume 0378, p.184.

Winter Remembered

As we draw this chapter on Winter to a close, we leave not just a record of storms and snowfalls, but a deeper understanding of how weather, in a place like Cork, becomes story. Here, winter is not simply the backdrop to people's lives, it is a force that shapes community, tests endurance, inspires folklore, and etches its presence into the very rhythm of the land.

What emerges most clearly from these recollections, from Ballydehob to Ballinglanna, from Boherboy to Fermoy, is that winter was not an inconvenience. It was an event, a reckoning, and sometimes, a tragedy. It could arrive with howling wind, as in the storm of 1839, which tore hay into rivers and homes into pieces. Or it could settle with eerie stillness, as in the great snows of 1853, 1892, and 1902, descending in the night and sealing entire households in place by morning.

And yet, amid the destruction and loss, these storms and snowfalls became oral monuments, remembered not only for their severity, but for what they revealed about the people who endured them.

From the first-hand accounts, we see the essential vulnerability of rural life: homes barely sealed against the cold, keyholes admitting snow, roofs rattling in the wind. Wells froze solid. Animals suffocated in snowdrifts. Trains stopped. Roads vanished. And yet, each story contains not just hardship, but humanity. Goats survived buried under snow thanks to a single breathing hole. Neighbours banded together to dig paths through twenty-foot drifts. Beggars were given shelter for weeks. Children played barefoot on thawing snowbanks in spring.

These are stories of adaptation, generosity, and survival. They are reminders that winter in Ireland was once not a season marked by indoor comfort and Christmas lights, but a looming threat to be faced communally. And so, while many of the stories begin with hardship, with the storm, the blackout, the freeze, they often end in solidarity. That is perhaps the most remarkable thing: winter's coldness gave rise to human warmth.

Cork's memory of winter also reveals a profound interdependence between people and the land. Storms were not experienced in isolation; they were part of a conversation between the natural and human world. In the storm of 1928, people could not return home for Christmas, a disruption felt spiritually as much as physically. In the snows of 1902 or 1856, people measured depth not in inches but in how long it blocked a chapel path, or how deep it covered their doors. Geography was never abstract in these stories, it was intimate. The well, the barn, the ditch where the sheep huddled, the banks where drifts gathered: all became part of the narrative.

And through it all, language itself becomes a form of shelter. The precision of the storytelling, the way the snow is described as entering through "slates," or being "as black as soot" when melted, tells us that these events were not forgotten. They were not merely survived but archived in the collective memory, passed down through grandmothers, school collectors, and local lore. One man remembered the storm so well, he could name the exact steep bank where a goat had survived for days. Another remembered the time "they couldn't take the baby to the chapel for six weeks." These are memories made sacred not just by survival, but by their continued telling.

Winter, then, becomes a kind of cultural watermark. Each generation remembers "the big snow," each village has its own year of disaster or resilience. The year of the blocked bridge. The year the priest couldn't say Mass. The year sheep were found breathing beneath the snow. These events are not merely meteorological, they are moral, emotional, and social markers, shaping how communities understood time, place, and each other.

Importantly, we also see how these winters did not strike evenly. The stories reflect the inequities of rural hardship, houses without proper windows, families without stored food, animals unattended because their owners lacked tools or help. Some had turf and survived; others did not. Some could melt snow for water, others had nothing to boil it with. These stories also remind us of a subsistence economy, where bread was a rarity, and families depended on potatoes, sour milk, or Indian meal gruel. In such a context, weather was not just a nuisance. It was the difference between comfort and catastrophe.

And yet, the tone is not one of complaint. It is one of record, often even humour. In one tale, a workman brings a nurse in a pannier during a snowstorm, only to have her fall through it on the way. In another, children play barefoot by the thawing snowbanks. This quiet stoicism, this way of laughing at hardship without mocking its severity, is a deeply Irish mode of storytelling, resilient, unpretentious, and profoundly communal.

Looking back on these winter tales, we see more than survival. We see a culture that made meaning out of difficulty. Weather, in Cork's tradition, was not random. It was a force that brought families together, slowed time, interrupted routine, and in doing so, created moments worth remembering. People measured their lives not by wealth or ease, but by whether they were "alive this time twelve months", or whether their animals had survived the storm, or whether their child had lived to see the christening.

As this chapter ends, we are left not just with images of snowdrifts and storms, but with a new understanding of how winter, in Cork, became history, not in books, but in barns, ballads, and memory. These accounts preserve a worldview in which the land and the weather are not backdrops but participants. A world in which the goat bleating from under the drift is not just a quirky tale, but a symbol of endurance. A world where even the smallest story, a blocked door, a melted candle, a blackened kettle, is worth passing on.

That is the heart of tradition: not just the event itself, but the memory of how we got through it. In today's world of central heating, weather alerts, and cleared roads, the hardships of these winters may seem distant. But the values they reveal, community, memory, self-reliance, and shared resilience, are as relevant now as ever. To read these winter stories is to enter a different tempo of life, one where the seasons truly mattered, and where every storm told a story worth keeping. In Cork, winter was cold, but the people were not.

7

The Origins of Christmas in Ireland

Long before the sound of Christian bells echoed through Irish valleys, and centuries before the Christ child was cradled in manger scenes across the land, the sacred groves of oak stirred with ritual. In the shadows of cairns and cromlechs, beneath mistletoe-laced boughs, the Druids of Ireland moved through a world alive with spirits, symbols, and seasonal rites. Though time has weathered their memory, and conquest has scattered their songs, fragments of their beliefs remain - in stone circles, in folktales, in midwinter customs that linger still.

To this historian, the Irish Druid is an elusive, mythic figure; to the folklorist, they were priests, poets, healers, and diviners, and their beliefs that shaped early Irish spiritual life. What little we know comes not from monuments or scripture, but from echoes: classical writers, bardic verse, and ritual practices that outlived theology. Most intriguing is how fragments of Druidic reverence, such as the cutting of mistletoe, were absorbed into the fabric of Christian Christmas, becoming playful custom while retaining shadows of ancient awe. Higgins (1827), writes:

The Druid Festival of Christmas

The festival of the twenty-fifth of December was celebrated by the Druids in Britain and Ireland with great fires lighted on the tops of the hills. This festival was repeated on the twelfth day, or on what we call the Epiphany. In some parts, the fires are still continued. We have not now remaining any documents to inform us what amongst the British Druids was the object or name of this festival, but perhaps we may gather it from circumstances.

The order of Druids, I scarcely need observe, was as common in France as in the British Isles. Christmas in France is called *Noel*; this word is, in fact, the Hebrew or Chaldee word *nule*. But if this be in the Chaldee dialect, the last letter may be emphatic, as it is in the word *mlc-e, the king*. In this case, it may mean *the parturition*; or it may be simply the verb *pariri*, to bring forth. In Irish, Christmas Day is called *Nolagh*. The name of Christmas Day in Cornish is *Nadelig*; in Armorican, *Nadelek*; in the Gael, *Nollig*.

The evergreens, and particularly the mistletoe, which are used all over the country, and even in London, in this festival, betray its Druidical origin. These had evidently nothing to do with Christianity.

Amongst the Gauls, more than a hundred years before the Christian era, in the district of Chartres, a festival was celebrated to the honour of the Virgin - *Virgini pariturae.*

In the year 1747, a Mithraic monument was found at Oxford, on which is exhibited a female nursing an infant. Stukeley has made a dissertation on this monument, which he shews to be a memorial of the birth of Mithra in the night of light.

The Protestant ought to recollect that his mode of keeping Christmas Day is only a small part of the old festival as it yet exists amongst the followers of the Romish Church. Theirs is a remnant of the old *Etruscan* worship of the Virgin and Child, - the Goddess *Nurtia* (whence our *nurse*). And the proof of this may be seen in Gorius's *Tuscan Antiquities*, where the reader will find a print of an old Etruscan Goddess with the child in her arms. No doubt the Romish Church would have claimed her for a Madonna, but most unluckily she has her name, *Nurtia*, in Etruscan letters, on her arm, after the Etruscan practice. This was a great festival with the Persians, who, in very early times, celebrated the birth of their God - Mithra. It was the custom of the Heathens, long before the birth of Christ, to celebrate the birthdays of their Gods. This was the example which the Christians, I think not very wisely, followed.

Amongst these ancient festivals, Christmas Day is perhaps the most curious. The assertion here made that this is nothing more than a remnant of the worship of the Druids, at first will startle the imagination of many persons; but whether the reader be a follower of the Roman Church, or a Protestant, if his understanding be not completely blinded by superstition, he will instantly see that the appointment, by the rulers of the Church, of a day for any particular ceremony, whether they acted from a true or a mistaken reason in selecting the day, cannot seriously affect the question of the truth of Christianity. It is a well-known fact, which the antiquarian divines of the Protestant or the Roman Church will not deny, that at the time when the festivals were settled, great feuds and even civil wars took place respecting them, before they were determined.

The monks of the Roman and Greek Churches were in those times the principal actors in these matters; they were few of them in orders, they were the remnants of the sect of the Essenes converted to Christianity, and much degraded and corrupted from their excellent predecessors in the time of Philo. It is not necessary to enter into this question here, but it may be shewn that there is no little probability, besides the tradition of the

Church, that the inscription noticed before upon the pedestal of the colossal statue of Elias, under the cupola of St. Peter at Rome, is true - *Elias Fundator Ordinis Carmelitarum.*

From Elias came the Essenes, and from the Essenes the Carmelite monks, who were in fact Christian Essenes. These people, in the early and Middle Ages of the Church, retained very little of the character given them by Philo and Josephus; they had sunk with the prevailing degradation of the human species. If they had not done so, human nature would not have become degraded; their exception alone would have prevented it.

These Essenes in Egypt, Persia, and other places, had probably given in to the prevailing adoration of the heavenly bodies, previously to the time of Philo; and when they became converts to Christianity, they formed an odd mixture of the two religions. Their first religion, in its origin and history, was forgotten, and their new one not learned. They were probably zealous devotees, but as ignorant as the lowest of the hermits and mendicant orders of the present Italians. The grade in society of many of these people, no educated member of the Roman communion requires teaching.[62]

As we trace the journey of the mistletoe from sacred branch to festive bough, we find in its survival a story of continuity: how old faiths whisper beneath new songs, and how winter, in Ireland, always carried more than one meaning. The following is taken from Sanderson's 1895 *Story of St Patrick*.

The Druidical Religion of Ireland

> Great were their deeds, their passions, and their sports;
> With clay and stone
> They piled on strath and shore those mystic forts,
> Nor yet o'erthrown;
> On cairn-crowned hills they held their council courts;
> While youths alone,
> With giant dogs, explored the elk resorts,
> And brought them down.
>
> The Druids' altar and the Druids' creed
> We scarce can trace.
> There is not left an undisputed deed
> Of all that race,
> Save their majestic song, which hath their speed,

---

[62] Godfrey Higgins, The Celtic Druids (London: Hunter, 1827), pp.162-164.

> And strength and grace;
> In that sole song they live and love and bleed -
> It bears them on thro' space.
>
> T. D. McGee

There are no definite accounts of the religious rites practised by the pagan Irish, but there are several allusions which, though vague, plainly show that such rites existed, and that it was one of the functions of the Druids to perform them.

These Druids were a class of priests corresponding to the Magi, or wise men, of the ancient Persians, and druidism was the name usually given to the religious system of the ancient Gauls and Britons.

The word Druid is thought to be derived from the Greek word *drus*, an oak. Groves of oak were their chosen retreat, and whatever grew on that tree was thought to be a gift from heaven, especially the mistletoe, under which fair ones still enjoy a kiss at Christmas. Wherever the mistletoe was found growing on an oak in those ancient times, it was cut with a golden knife by a priest clad in a white robe, and two white bulls were sacrificed upon the spot. The Druids called it "all heal," and its virtues were considered to be very great.

The mistletoe was only regarded with reverence when found growing on the sacred oak, the tree of one of the gods of the ancient Britons. These druidic rites were maintained under the Romans, Jutes, Saxons, and Angles.

But how and when the mistletoe became ingrafted on the greatest festival of the Christian world is not yet apparent, and is evidently lost in the darkness of the dim and misty past. The mistletoe also appears in the Scandinavian mythology, in which an arrow formed from the mistletoe is represented as a sure weapon of success in a contest with an adversary.

The custom of kissing under a suspended bough of the mistletoe has come down from the druidic days and is likely to survive to the end of time, as it has survived the faith of the ancient Britons.

Possibly the popularity of the rite has had much to do with its survival. In some parts of England, if a man neglects to provide the evergreens for the Christmas decoration, he loses the privilege of kissing any maid or dame he catches under the mistletoe bough. This pleasant holiday custom has found expression in the following lively lines:

> On Christmas eve the bells were rung;
> On Christmas eve the mass was sung;
> That only night in all the year
> Saw the stoled priest the chalice rear;

> The damsel donned her kirtle sheen,
> The hall was dressed with holly green;
> Forth to the wood the merrymen go,
> To gather in the mistletoe.

The Druids made the cutting of the mistletoe an occasion of solemn religious ceremonies, terminating often in extreme barbarity.[63]

Pepper, in his The Ancient Mode of Celebrating Christmas in Ireland (1829), reflects the Christian Christmas in Ireland.

Reflection

The hallowed period of Christmas was celebrated by the ancient Irish with great pomp and festivity. In Flemming's *History of Ancient Irish Customs*, we have an elaborate account of the festivity and amusement that prevailed at this season of gayety and mirth, which was the very millennium of hospitality and social intercourse. On Christmas eve, the village maidens repaired to the groves to gather ivy and holly, which they generally wove into garlands, for the decoration of the village church, and their own apartments. At seven o'clock in the evening, the church bells greeted "old father Christmas" with a merry peal; then the immense "Christmas candles" were lit up, the large block of ash blazed on the smiling hearth, the enormous wassail bowl of whiskey punch smoked upon the antique oak table, and after the priest had said grace, and offered up a prayer of gratulation and thanksgiving, the bards had chaunted a carol on their harps, the feudal chieftain caused the door of his spacious hall to be thrown open, who, proud of his vassals and dependants, with a smile as cheerful as his hearth, and a heart as open as the portals of his castle, bade all that entered welcome, and to those that departed an affectionate adieu.

After feasting on fish and fruits, the wassail bowl went round briskly, and the bards then raised the festive strains. So late as the sixteenth century, it was the custom in the county of Kerry for the poor retainers of the chief to carry about to the neighbouring houses, with the wassail-cup an image of our Saviour, together with a quantity of roasted apples, steeped in a large tankard of mead, so that all might be reminded of the birth of the Messiah, and have an opportunity of drinking to the health of the chieftain and his lady. In those remote days, a wassail bowl, or cup, was placed on the tables of Lords, as well as on those of the Abbots, whose doors were ever open for the reception of the poor and the stranger.

---

[63] J. Sanderson, *Story of St Patrick* (New York: Ketcham, 1895), pp.44-45.

In Archdal's Monasticon, there is an engraving of the wassail bowl which belonged to the abbey of Kildare. The inside (which held two quarts) was furnished with eight pegs, at equal distances one below the other, in conformity with the sumptuary ordinances of the Prior, to repress visitants from excess in drinking. This measurement allowed of half a pint of strong wine to each person. This antique cup, we believe, is still in the possession of his Grace the Duke of Leinster.

At midnight, the lord and the peasant repaired to the church to offer their devotions and hear a solemn mass; but after two o'clock on Christmas morning, devotions and austerities gave way to pleasure and rejoicing. On their coming home from church, the wassail bowl, which, though rudely shaped from Galway marble, contained liquor fit for the lips of the Indian Bacchus, and worthy to celebrate his return from conquest. The wassail liquor was composed of wine, brandy, some water, spices of various kinds, and roasted apples, which floated in triumph on its foaming top. Music and song always ushered in Christmas morning. The swain sung his serenade ditty under his mistress's window - the harper allured sweet notes from his music-breathing strings, and the discordant horn and shrill pipe contributed sounds, if not melody, to the concert. The Christmas day was like a day of victory; every house and church were as green as spring. The laurel, plucked by the hand of beauty, and the holly, with its scarlet berries shining like fireflies, decorated the altar of hospitality. On that day, the eve of Christ, all distinctions of rank and station were forgotten at the great dinner in the chieftain's hall, where the "tables groaned with the weight of the feast."

But now the good old custom of celebrating Christmas, with profuse hospitality, is almost dispensed with in Ireland; and alas! the song of the bard, nor the voice of merriment, no longer resounds in the mansions of the Irish nobility. These heartless absentees, instead of diffusing the blessings of benevolence and hospitality among the poor tenantry from whom they derive their incomes, are revelling in luxuries in Paris or Rome, and regardless of the miseries which they do not feel, they look like the bloated gods of Epicurus, with unconcern on the privations and sufferings of a brave peasantry, experiencing, while labouring for the support of these voluptuaries, the extremities of want and the bitterness of cold.[64]

---

[64] George Pepper (ed), The Ancient Mode of Celebrating Christmas in Ireland, *The Irish Shield and Monthly Milesian*, vol. 1, 1829, pp.5-7.

8

Commerce in Cork

Cork's commercial history is one of transformation: from a marsh-island settlement negotiated by timber bridges and tidal channels, into a major Atlantic port whose butter and beef once fed empires. The rhythms of trade shaped its streets, its institutions, its social life, and its cultural confidence. By the mid-eighteenth century, the city was "by far the most important" of Ireland's county towns.[65] Yet behind that achievement lay a much older urban landscape, one vividly captured in the late-seventeenth-century map on which this chapter is partly based.

What follows is a study of Cork's commercial evolution over two and a half centuries. It traces the early marsh-island geography visible on the seventeenth-century plan; the rise of the beef and butter trades; the creation of markets, mills, bridges, and canals; the expansion of shipping and global connections; the leisure and cultural worlds generated by mercantile wealth; and the continuation of that commercial energy into the nineteenth and early twentieth centuries, as seen in advertisements, personal testimony, and the built environment.

The late-seventeenth-century map of Cork (Figure 12), the earliest detailed plan of the town and its commercial arteries, shows a settlement suspended between land and water. The city is drawn not as a single mass, but as a constellation of islands in the branching River Lee: North Island, South Island, Hammond's Marsh, and the smaller protrusions around the Sand Key. Each island is interlaced with quays, lanes, markets, and bridges. The map's visual logic makes clear that Cork was shaped by water long before industry.

Hammond's Marsh occupies the northwest portion of the map: a large, irregularly shaped island bounded by tidal channels, dotted with narrow lanes and plots that suggest early reclamation. Even in the seventeenth century, this marshland was being transformed into a zone of commercial production. Warehouses and yards clustered near the water; ropewalks, tanneries, and timber stores lay close by. The map captures this

---

[65] John Hobson Matthews, "Notes and Queries," 8th series, vol. 11, January–June 1897, p.54.

sense of a city actively making land as it made itself, later described as Cork's "marsh-forging, quay-stretching urban metabolism."[66]

To the east lies the Sand Key, a slim spit of land protruding into the channel, its position suggestive of a natural breakwater for shipping. The map depicts small structures and mooring points here, indicating its early use as a landing or storage space. It would later become a crucial node in the expansion of the city's quays.

North and South Main Streets appear on the seventeenth-century plan as the commercial spine of the city, aligned along the two principal islands. Their narrowness and density, every plot filled, every lane connected to a quay, speak of a town oriented toward river traffic.

Goods came in by boat and left by boat. Carts could traverse the bridges, but water transport was often faster and more reliable. Three early bridges connect the islands: simple structures compared to the eighteenth-century stone spans that would replace them, but vital in binding together a community whose life was defined by tide, mud, and channel. The map shows Cork not as a fortified stronghold but as a trading organism; its defences are present, but its orientation is unmistakably commercial.

Crucially, the map also shows the earliest traceable market zones: the Market House near South Main Street, smaller butcher stalls near the shambles, and the lanes leading toward the medieval Red Abbey, an area known even then for milling and grain processing.[67]

Taken together, the map reveals a proto-commercial city: one whose topography was as much economic as geographic; a settlement whose future prosperity was already inscribed in the shape of its channels, quays, and reclaimed marshlands.

The seventeenth-century map captures the city at a moment of transition. Over the next several decades, external forces accelerated its transformation. The Cromwellian and Williamite wars, the growth of the English navy, and the expansion of Atlantic plantation economies all created heightened demand for provisions, beef, butter, salted fish, pork, hides, and tallow, the very products for which Cork was geographically and agriculturally poised.

---

[66] David Dickson, *Old World Colony: Cork and South Munster 1630–1830* (Cork: Cork University Press, 1947), p.113.
[67] T. F. McCarthy, "Markets and Trade in Seventeenth-Century Cork," *Journal of Munster Studies* 9, no. 2 (1998), pp22-35.

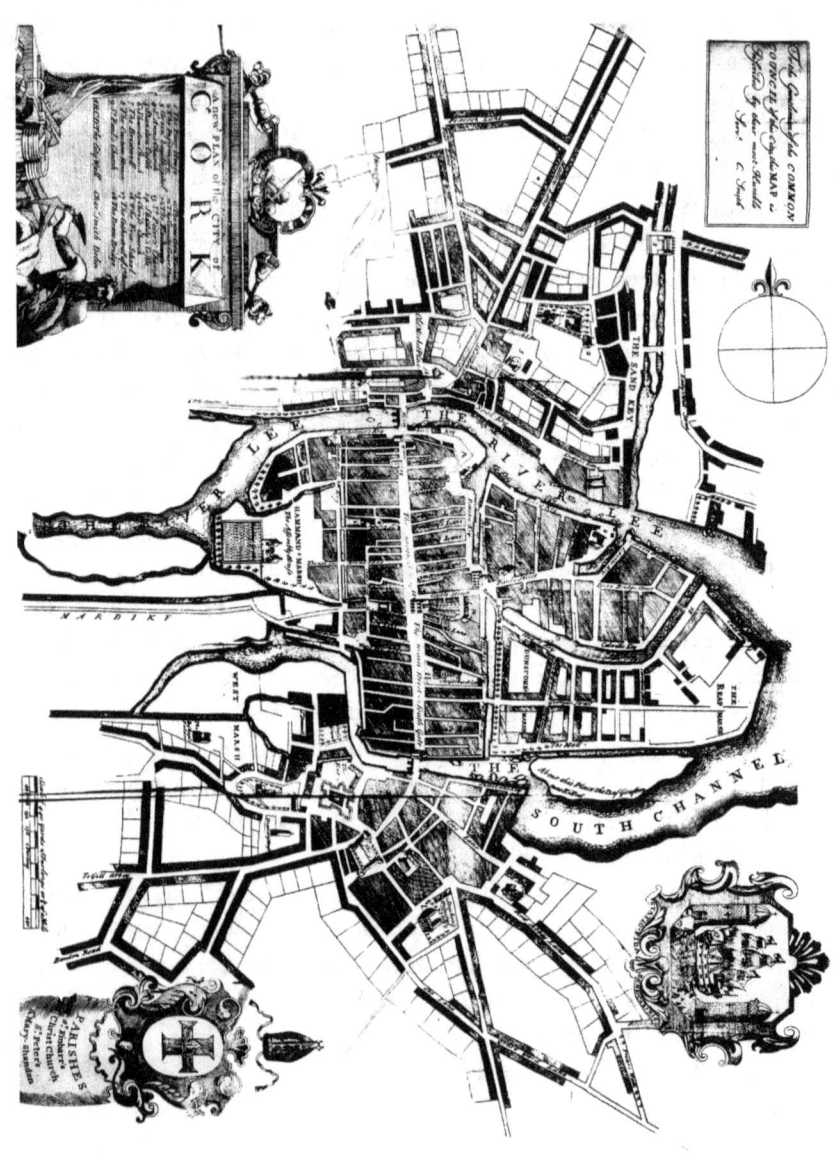

Figure 12. Map of Cork City, Charles Smith, *The antient and present state of the county and city of Cork*, vol. 1 (Dublin: Reilly, 1750).

Cork's hinterland, the dairy heartlands of Muskerry, the cattle-rich plains of east Limerick, the butter farms of West Cork, fed directly into the city's early markets. Herds were driven along ancient drover routes, across narrow bridges, and through muddy lanes to reach the quays. Here, as the seventeenth-century map shows, slaughter yards and salting houses were situated close to the river channels for easy export.

As early as the 1680s, Cork was emerging as a major provisioning centre for the English Royal Navy and merchant fleets.[68] The tidal channels of the Lee allowed ships to berth close to the urban core, while the city's marsh-island structure created natural clusters of industrial activity: tanning on Hammond's Marsh, milling near the Red Abbey, and storage on the Sand Key.

By the early eighteenth century, commercial confidence was manifest in new civic structures. The construction of the two stone bridges in 1712 and 1713, replacing earlier timber ones shown on the seventeenth-century map, symbolised Cork's transition from marsh settlement to substantial port town. The Green-coat Hospital (founded 1715), new barracks (1719), and the rebuilding of the cathedral (1725–1735) were all financed, directly or indirectly, by mercantile wealth.

By the mid-eighteenth century, Cork's commercial expansion had reached a new scale. As John Hobson Matthews later summarised:

> Of county towns Cork, in the middle of the eighteenth century, was by far the most important… owing to its admirable harbour, and to the great trade which had sprung up in beef, it had considerably outstripped both Waterford and Limerick…. 'From Michaelmas to Christmas,' wrote a traveller, 'a stranger would imagine it was the slaughter-house of Ireland.[69]

This was no exaggeration. Tens of thousands of cattle were driven annually into the city. Salting houses operated day and night. The smell of curing beef and tanning hides filled the air. Cork beef was exported to Britain, Portugal, Spain, and especially the Caribbean, where it provisioned plantations and naval fleets.

Butter, too, became a cornerstone of Cork's trade. Even before the establishment of the Butter Exchange in the 1770s, firkins were being exported in vast quantities. The butter tasters, inspectors appointed to

---

[68] Michael O'Neill, *Provisioning the Empire: Irish Ports and Global Trade, 1650–1750* (Manchester: Manchester Unversity Press, 2014), pp.77-82.
[69] Matthews (1897), p.54.

grade quality, emerged informally in this period before becoming institutionalised later.[70]

The map's seventeenth-century marsh-island layout helps explain this rise: proximity to tidal channels meant that commodities could be transported efficiently by water. The very geography recorded on the map was a strategic asset.

Cork in the eighteenth century was not particularly beautiful. As the *Notes & Queries* extract observes: 'Except the great natural beauty of its situation, it exhibited little or nothing to attract the eye of the artist, but it had all the animation of a gay, prosperous, and improving town.'[69] Yet its built environment, marked by new bridges, a new exchange, corn markets, and widened quays, reflected commercial ambition. The city's Protestant mercantile elite financed theatres, assembly rooms, coffee-houses, promenades, and bowling greens.

Music flourished. Corelli, Handel, and Italian airs were performed in drawing rooms: 'Besides the public concerts, there are several private ones… Italic airs saluting his ears… Corelli is a name in more mouths than many of our Lord-Lieutenants.' Commerce produced culture; barrels of butter paid for violins and harpsichords.

The eighteenth-century city retained much of the underlying topography visible on the seventeenth-century map but infused it with new commercial infrastructure. Canals were cut to link the channels of the Lee, enabling goods to be moved through the urban core. Many were later infilled to create the streets we know today, but their watery origins remain visible in the irregular shapes of bridges and quays.

The Exchange became the nerve centre of mercantile life. Around it developed a dense network of shambles, corn markets, and butter markets. The creation of the Butter Exchange, the world's largest by the late eighteenth century, was a direct outgrowth of the early butter trade already hinted at on the seventeenth-century map's commercial waterfronts.

Meanwhile, the mixed religious landscape of Cork, with Catholic chapels, Protestant churches, a French church, a Quaker meetinghouse, and Presbyterian and Anabaptist chapels, speaks to a cosmopolitan merchant community. The city that once struggled against tide and marsh had become one of the busiest commercial hubs in the Atlantic world.

---

[70] Ciarán O'Driscoll, "The Cork Butter Market, 1700–1800," *Irish Economic and Social History* 18 (1991), pp.31-49.

Figure 13. The Corn Exchange, Cork.

The nineteenth century brought both continuity and transformation. Cork remained fundamentally a provisioning port, but new forces, steam power, iron shipbuilding, railways, and the rise of modern consumer culture, reshaped the commercial landscape.

The deep-water quays at Passage and Queenstown (Cóbh) became major nodes for shipping. Coal-yards multiplied, feeding steam engines on ships and in factories. Cork shipyards, once focused on wooden vessels, adapted to hybrid and iron-hulled ships. Railways further integrated the city's hinterland. Dairy, grain, and livestock reached Cork faster and in greater volume than ever before. Rural buyers travelled to the city for goods unavailable in smaller market towns.

The intensification of trade is vividly reflected in the advertising pages of Cork's nineteenth-century newspapers. These advertisements, whose placeholders appear here for later insertion, capture the texture of daily commercial life (Figure 14).

```
        CHRISTMAS AND NEW YEAR.

    PRESENTS!    PRESENTS!!    PRESENTS!!!

EW PURSES.                        OAK and WALNUT STATIONEY CASES.
)RTABLE WRITING CASES.            OAK and WALNUT INKSTANDS.
ADIES' WRITING DESKS, in Leather. WALNUT ENVELOPE CASES and BLOT-
)MBINED DESK and DESPATCH BOXES.    TERS.
ESPATCH BOXES, in Morocco and Russia.  ELEGANT PAPER CUTTERS.
LEGANT ALBUMS and SCRAP-BOOKS.    POSTAGE SCALES, for Letters and Parcels.
ADIES' BIJOU MEMORANDUM BOOKS.    IVORY and SILVER PENCILS and PEN-
 ATER COLOR BOXES, elegantly fitted.  HOLDERS.
IL COLOR TIN BOXES fitted complete. IVORY and SILVER PENHOLDERS, and
LAYING CARDS, DE LA RUE'S New       GOLD PENS.
 Patterns.                        TORTOISE-SHELL and CARD CASES.
ICROSCOPES, TELESCOPES, and OPERA PEARL and IVORY POCKET TABLETS.
 GLASSES.                         NEW RESERVOIR PENHOLDERS, to contain
ERMAN BRONZES, in great variety.    Ink.
TEREOSCOPES and SLIDES.

    Many of the above can be sent by Post, or to any Railway Station, at a very trifling Cost.
          COUNTRY ORDERS RECEIVE SPECIAL ATTENTION.

                  FRANCIS GUY
```

Figure 14. The Cork Herald, vol. 4, no. 36.9, 24 December 1859.

This period saw the rise of large-scale drapery houses, tea and sugar importers, grocers advertising Christmas goods, and merchants selling everything from preserved fruits to ironmongery. Such adverts mirror the consumer expansion associated with Victorian middle-class culture.

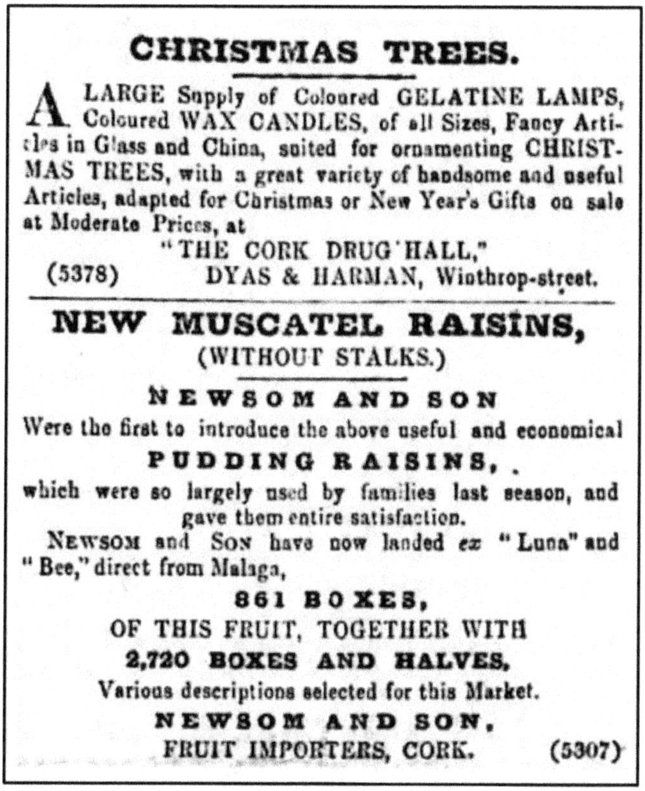

> **CHRISTMAS TREES.**
>
> A LARGE Supply of Coloured GELATINE LAMPS, Coloured WAX CANDLES, of all Sizes, Fancy Articles in Glass and China, suited for ornamenting CHRISTMAS TREES, with a great variety of handsome and useful Articles, adapted for Christmas or New Year's Gifts on sale at Moderate Prices, at
> "THE CORK DRUG HALL,"
> (5378) DYAS & HARMAN, Winthrop-street.
>
> **NEW MUSCATEL RAISINS,**
> (WITHOUT STALKS.)
> **NEWSOM AND SON**
> Were the first to introduce the above useful and economical
> **PUDDING RAISINS,**
> which were so largely used by families last season, and gave them entire satisfaction.
> NEWSOM and SON have now landed ex "Luna" and "Bee," direct from Malaga,
> **861 BOXES,**
> OF THIS FRUIT, TOGETHER WITH
> **2,720 BOXES AND HALVES,**
> Various descriptions selected for this Market.
> **NEWSOM AND SON,**
> FRUIT IMPORTERS, CORK. (5307)

Figure 15. Cork Constitution, Monday 24 December 1860.

The commercial tempo heightens in the 1860s (Figure 15). Here, seasonal demand is evident: Christmas food orders, holiday timetables, shipping notices, and charitable distributions. Retail commerce was becoming increasingly organised and heavily advertised, shaped by festive rhythms.

The 1870s generated some of the richest surviving advertisements (Figures 16 & 17). These typically feature butter quotations, grain prices, drapery sales, shipping arrivals, and notices of trains facilitating holiday travel. They also reveal an expanding entertainment culture: theatre programmes, concerts, and exhibitions.

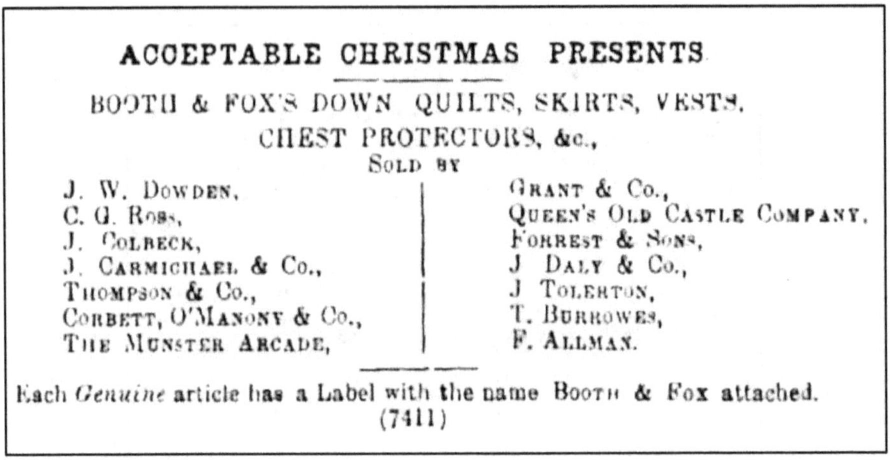

```
ACCEPTABLE CHRISTMAS PRESENTS
BOOTH & FOX'S DOWN QUILTS, SKIRTS, VESTS,
           CHEST PROTECTORS, &c.,
                   SOLD BY
J. W. DOWDEN,                 GRANT & CO.,
C. G. ROSS,                   QUEEN'S OLD CASTLE COMPANY,
J. COLBECK,                   FORREST & SONS,
J. CARMICHAEL & CO.,          J DALY & CO.,
THOMPSON & CO.,               J TOLERTON,
CORBETT, O'MANONY & CO.,      T. BURROWES,
THE MUNSTER ARCADE,           F. ALLMAN.

Each Genuine article has a Label with the name BOOTH & FOX attached.
                       (7411)
```

```
            RACES AT LAPLANDS.

         ST. STEPHEN'S DAY, 1870.

  THE shortest Route to these Races is by the
      ROCHESTOWN STATION on the Pas-
  sage Railway.
     Third Class Return Tickets, 6d.  Trains stop
  every hour as required.                  7515
```

Figure 16. Cork Constitution, Saturday 24 December 1870, p.1.
Figure 17. Cork Daily Herald, Saturday 24 December 1870.

By the 1880s, new sectors dominated newspaper advertising. Insurance companies, bicycle sellers, sewing machine agents, photographic studios, and patent medicine vendors are all present, signs of a modernising urban consumer economy. The wealth generated by trade shaped Cork's social world. The great mercantile families, the Conners, Newmans, Harleys, and Sainthills, among others, patronised music, theatre, and philanthropy. Theatres, coffee-houses, reading rooms, and assembly rooms flourished. This social refinement had deep eighteenth-century roots.[71] By the nineteenth century, these traditions had expanded. The Athenaeum, Mechanics' Institute, and various literary societies reflected the aspirations of a prosperous middle class. Women became central to commercial sociability.

---

[71] Matthews (1897), p.54.

The growth of drapery houses, millinery establishments, and piano dealers reflected a gendered consumer culture in which women shaped household purchasing decisions. Newspaper adverts emphasise this shift, especially in the 1890s. Cork's commercial world was not only about ships and markets; it was also about social presentation, leisure, and taste.

By 1900, Cork was deeply embedded in global networks. Its port handled traffic from Britain, North America, France, Spain, and South America. Telegraphy, steam transport, and railways allowed merchants to track prices and ship goods with unprecedented speed.

At the turn of the century, Cork's advertising landscape vividly reflected its transformation into a modern, consumer-oriented city. It revealed a thriving trade in imported luxury goods, ranging from exotic fruits and fine spices to wines and festive indulgences, designed to satisfy the refined tastes and growing seasonal expectations of the emerging middle class. Department stores promoted fashionable wares such as Parisian modes, signalling an increasing influence of continental style on local tastes.

Meanwhile, the emergence of cycle dealers and motor-related services illustrated the rise of mechanized transport, while advertisements for gas and electrical fittings highlighted the spread of modern utilities into homes and businesses. Music shops selling gramophones and sheet music offered both entertainment and cultural sophistication, pointing to the commercialization of leisure. Expanded railway timetables were also widely publicized, reflecting both improved mobility and the integration of regional trade with national and international networks. Together, these ads depict a vibrant, consumer-oriented Cork firmly embedded in the rhythms of modernity and global exchange.

Commerce does not exist in abstraction; it lives through the experiences of individuals. One of the most evocative personal testimonies recounts the life of Patrick Hayes, who was born in County Cork over a century earlier. 'He remembers the French landing in Bantry Bay in 1798… sings long-forgotten patriotic ditties… can read and write without much difficulty… scarcely a grey hair… attends early Mass on Christmas Day.'[72] Hayes' life bridged the old marsh-island Cork of the seventeenth-century map and the modern Victorian port of railways, trams, and global trade. Born in the era of firkins and salted beef, he lived to see bicycles, electric lights, and a bustling retail culture. His memory of the French scare of 1798 connects to the broader context of Cork's military provisioning role; his longevity underscores the continuity of lived experience beneath the

---

[72] Matthews (1897), p.54.

city's dramatic commercial transformations. He is described walking in 'the coldest weather without an overcoat,' a man shaped by a world of physical labour and maritime climate. His "regiment of descendants" suggests the embeddedness of families like his in the fabric of Cork's commercial and social life.

9

Rupture

Christmas in Ireland is often imagined through the warm glow of candlelight, the hush of sacred song, the flicker of home and hearth. But beyond the festive peace, history reminds us that the season has also been a time of rupture, violence, and national anxiety.

Christmas Eve 1601: The Fall of Kinsale

As midnight approached on Christmas Eve 1601, the narrow lanes and salt-swept battlements of Kinsale fell eerily quiet. Far from the warmth of hearths or the joy of Christmas, the town bore witness to a moment of defeat, despair, and geopolitical reckoning, yet no bells rang for peace. Instead, the Spanish commander Don Juan del Águila surrendered the town of Kinsale to the English under Lord Mountjoy, bringing to a bitter end the most ambitious foreign intervention in Irish history - and delivering a deathblow to Gaelic Ireland's last great hope.[73]

The Battle of Kinsale, often remembered for its military implications, was also an emotional and symbolic trauma for the people of County Cork, felt most acutely on what should have been the holiest night of the year.

The siege of Kinsale had dragged on for months. The Spanish forces, numbering around 3,500 men, had landed unexpectedly in late September 1601,[74] occupying the fortified port town with hopes of joining the Irish rebels to strike against English rule. But instead of finding Irish allies waiting, they were isolated - encircled by Mountjoy's forces and cut off from resupply.[75]

By December, cold, hunger, and disease gripped the town. Eyewitness accounts suggest even fresh water had become scarce.[76] The Spanish, weakened and demoralized, endured daily cannon fire and night

---

[73] Hiram Morgan, *Tyrone's Rebellion: The Outbreak of the Nine Years War in Tudor Ireland* (Woodbridge: Boydell, 1993), p.235.
[74] John McGurk, *Sir Henry Docwra, 1564–1631: Derry's Second Founder* (Dublin: Four Courts Press, 1997), p.151.
[75] Cyril Falls, *Elizabeth's Irish Wars* (Syracuse: Syracuse University Press, 1996), 247–248.
[76] Peter Berresford Ellis, *Hell or Connaught! The Cromwellian Colonisation of Ireland* (Belfast: Blackstaff, 1985), p.54.

raids. For the townspeople of Kinsale, Christmas that year was not a time of worship and feasting, but one of anxiety, occupation, and fear. Livestock had been slaughtered, markets had vanished, families fled or hid.

And then, on Christmas Eve, the Spanish - realising their Irish allies had failed to break through - surrendered.[77]

North of Kinsale, Hugh O'Neill and Hugh Roe O'Donnell were making the last desperate push to save the Spanish garrison. They had marched over 300 kilometres from Ulster in mid-winter, braving storms, boglands, and frost.[78]

On 3 January 1602, ten days after the Spanish surrendered, the Irish launched a final, desperate attack - only to be crushed in a swift English counter-charge.[79] The moment had passed. Kinsale had already fallen. And with it, the dream of a Catholic Gaelic Ireland.

For the people of County Cork, that Christmas marked more than a lost battle - it marked the beginning of profound and permanent change. The area had long been a cultural crossroads: a stronghold of Gaelic chiefs, a centre of maritime trade, and a region with deep religious traditions.[80]

But after 1601, English control intensified. Land was seized from Irish families and redistributed to Protestant settlers. Catholic worship, especially public Masses and feast days like Christmas, was increasingly driven underground.[81] Cork's winter festivals, once filled with Celtic and Catholic symbolism, were now shadowed by fear of surveillance and repression.

Yet the people persisted. Oral traditions, candlelit Masses in hidden glens, and songs sung quietly by the fire sustained the spirit of the season through adversity.[82]

In centuries to follow, Christmas in Cork would slowly return to joy. But in the early 17th century, each December carried the memory of that bitter eve - when Spanish soldiers laid down arms, Irish hopes collapsed, and the streets of Kinsale echoed not with carols but with the silence of defeat.

---

[77] Nicholas Canny, *Making Ireland British, 1580–1650* (Oxford: Oxford University Press, 2001), 87.
[78] Pádraig Lenihan, *Consolidating Conquest: Ireland 1603–1727* (London: Routledge, 2001), 11.
[79] J.H. O'Neill, "The Battle of Kinsale," *Irish Historical Studies* 6, no. 21 (1948): 23–42.
[80] Steven G. Ellis, *Tudor Ireland: Crown, Community and the Conflict of Cultures* (London: Longman, 1998), 184–186.
[81] Ciaran Brady, *The Chief Governors: The Rise and Fall of Reform Government in Tudor Ireland, 1536–1588* (Cambridge: Cambridge University Press, 1994), 211.
[82] Margaret MacCurtain and Donnchadh Ó Corráin, eds., *Women in Early Modern Ireland* (Dublin: Arlen, 1978), 101–102.

Modern historians still debate the broader significance of the battle. Some, like Hiram Morgan, see it as the natural end of an overreaching Gaelic rebellion,[83] while others argue that better coordination with the Spanish might have turned the tide.[84] Either way, Christmas 1601 stands out as a solemn pivot in Cork's - and Ireland's - past.

If you stroll Kinsale today during the festive season - past the harbour lit with Christmas lights or the old town walls decorated with wreaths - you walk atop centuries of history. You walk where Spanish soldiers once shivered on Christmas Eve. You walk where Irish chiefs dreamed of freedom - and lost it.

Yet Christmas returns, year after year, to Cork. And perhaps there is some grace in that - the endurance of light after darkness, of memory after silence, and of a people who, even in the face of conquest, kept their spirit burning like a candle in the window on Christmas night.

The Invasion of Ireland - Christmas 1796

In December 1796, as many Irish families prepared for the holy day, a French invasion fleet, estimated by various sources to be between 14,000 and 20,000 strong, approached the coast of Bantry Bay. The ballad that follows, composed in the weeks after, captures not only the military drama of the failed landing, but also a theological interpretation of divine intervention during one of Ireland's most politically fraught Christmases.

The poem that follows, entitled *The Invasion*, (written in January 1797), is not merely jingoistic celebration. It stands as a testament to the way ordinary life, even sacred time, is vulnerable to the storm of geopolitics. While candles were lit for the Christ child, they also flickered anxiously against the threat of war. The French, portrayed here with anti-republican venom, are cast not just as political enemies, but as enemies of God, scoffing at the nativity as the storm gathered.

As we consider the Irish Christmas across centuries, this episode reminds us: peace was never guaranteed, and even holy nights bore the tremor of distant drums.

---

[83] Morgan, *Tyrone's Rebellion*, 248–251.
[84] James McCavitt, *The Flight of the Earls* (Dublin: Gill & Macmillan, 2002), 66–69.

The Invasion

Now fair and strong the south-east blew,
 And high the billows rose;
The French fleet bounded o'er the main,
 Freighted with Erin's foes.

Oh! where was Hood, and where was Howe,
 And where Cornwallis then;
Where Colpoys, Bridport, or Pellew,
 And all their gallant men?

Nor skill nor courage aught avail,
 Against high Heaven's decrees;
The storm arose and closed our ports,
 A mist o'erspread the seas.

For not to feeble, mortal man,
 Did God his vengeance trust;
He raised his own tremendous arm,
 All-powerful as all just.
Now fierce and loud the tempest roared,
 And swept the quivering main;
And part go south, and part go west,
 And part the shore attain.

And trembling† on the boisterous wave,
 The shattered vessels lie;
The billows mounting o'er their heads,
 To kiss the bending sky.

"Arise, ye sons of Erin, rise,
 The Gaul is on the shore;
He comes, begrim'd with murder foul
 And red with royal gore."

The sons of Themis proudly drew
 The sword of justice bright;
And thirty thousand yeomen's swords
 Reflected back its light.

Now firm and bold her patriot sons
　　To Erin's coasts repair;
With ardent zeal they hold their march,
　　Their banners fill the air.

But not to Albion's navy bold,
　　Nor Erin's patriot band,
Did God his ministry depute
　　To save his favored land.

In Bantry's deep‡ and rocky bay,
　　The hostile navy rode;
And now arrived the festal hour
　　When earth beheld her God.

The impious crews,‖ with anxious eyes
　　Gazed on each verdant plain;
And mocked and scoffed the holy time
　　With many a jest profane.
They laughed to scorn the sacred hour,
　　That saw their Saviour's birth;
And dared the Lord they would not serve
　　To cast them on the earth.

But God beheld their impious pride,
　　And, lo! His anger woke;
He bade the elements divide,
　　And gave His tempest stroke.

The rolling thunder rent the skies,
　　The lightning smote the deep;
The haughty fleet in ruin lies,
　　And dares no longer keep.

Each gallant bark that proudly bore
　　The arms of France and fame,
Now shattered lies on Erin's shore,
　　Or sinks in wreaths of flame.

Then loud and deep the tempest poured,
　　The seamen shrieked in vain;
The whirlwinds howled, the billows roared,
　　And swept them from the main.

O'er Bantry's Bay the wild wind passed,
The stormy night was o'er;
The morning dawned serene at last,
But France was seen no more.

Thus. Heaven preserved the favoured isle,
Thus Erin's God was known;
He smiled upon her once again,
And claimed her for His own.

Then let the sons of Erin raise
Their voices to the sky;
And sing, through everlasting days,
The Lord that heard their cry.

10

A State is Born - Christmas 1922 in Cork

On the 6th of December 1922, just weeks before Christmas, Ireland entered a new era with the proclamation of the Irish Free State (Saorstát Éireann). For the people of Cork - a city with deep republican traditions and one still reeling from the traumas of war, civil conflict, and the burning of its heart by British forces in 1920 - this December was unlike any before it. Christmas lights flickered in shopfronts amid a lingering haze of gunpowder smoke and uncertainty. While carollers rehearsed in parishes, government ministers debated oaths of allegiance. And while children wrote hopeful letters to Santa Claus, the nation stepped cautiously into a new, fragile independence.

On paper, the Irish Free State was born in triumph. On 6 December 1921, the Anglo-Irish Treaty had been signed in London, and exactly a year later, it came into force. Yet in Cork - as in much of Ireland - the reaction was conflicted. While some viewed it as a new dawn, many considered it a bitter compromise. The proclamation was issued in London by King George V, not in Dublin, and certainly not in Cork, reminding many nationalists that true independence remained elusive.[85]

In the streets of Cork, the atmosphere was one of cautious festivity. The city was recovering from its central role in the War of Independence and the ongoing Civil War that followed. For some Corkonians, particularly those with pro-Treaty sympathies, the establishment of the Free State represented the first tangible outcome of generations of nationalist struggle. For others - especially anti-Treaty republicans - 6 December was a day of mourning. They saw the Treaty as a betrayal of the Irish Republic proclaimed in 1916 and reinforced by the First Dáil in 1919.

As historian David Gwynn observed in his account of the period, the early Free State was defined less by peace than by uneasy transition.[86] In Cork, this was especially pronounced. The city had been a major IRA stronghold, and many of its fighters now opposed the Treaty. By Christmas, the Cork No. 1 Brigade was operating underground or in the hills of West Cork, waging guerrilla resistance.

---

[85] Thomas Mohr, "Law and the Foundation of the Irish State on 6 December 1922," *Irish Jurist* 60 (2018): 1–22.
[86] David Gwynn, *The Irish Free State, 1922–1927* (Dublin: Talbot Press, 1928), 3–25.

Despite the political upheaval, Christmas still arrived. Cork's streets in December 1922 bore the hallmarks of tradition - Christmas masses, pantomimes at the Opera House, seasonal shopfronts, and railway workers sending turkeys home in parcels. Beneath the decorations, tension pulsed. The assassination of TD Seán Hales on 7 December, just one day after the proclamation, was a stark reminder that civil conflict raged.[87]

Newspapers such as the Cork Examiner carried both Christmas advertisements and dispatches about executions, raids, and reprisals. People queued for flour and sugar while rumours circulated about Republican attacks on infrastructure. The lines between Christmas peace and political violence blurred, and Cork's citizens learned to celebrate even as they mourned.

To understand why this moment mattered, one must consider what was actually proclaimed on 6 December. The Irish Free State Constitution, passed by the Third Dáil and ratified by the British Parliament, set out the structures of governance for a self-governing dominion within the British Commonwealth, similar to Canada.[88] Its preamble and first articles emphasized Irish sovereignty while maintaining symbolic ties to the Crown, most notably through the Oath of Allegiance.

For many in Cork, the Oath - sworn "to be faithful to His Majesty King George V" - was anathema. Among local anti-Treaty IRA units and Republican families, the Christmas of 1922 brought not joy, but betrayal. As Laura Cahillane has written, the Constitution was an exercise in compromise: it tried to satisfy both the Irish desire for autonomy and the British insistence on unity and dominion structure.[89] But for many Cork republicans, nothing short of a full republic would suffice.

Yet it's also important to recognize the stability and legitimacy the Constitution offered. As legal scholar Thomas Mohr argues, while the Free State's birth was shaped by imperial influence, the 1922 Constitution still marked an important step toward Irish legislative independence.[90]

While Ireland as a whole struggled to adapt to its new statehood, Cork remained a frontline in the civil war between pro- and anti-Treaty forces. In the weeks surrounding Christmas, the National Army intensified its control of the region. Raids were frequent, and tensions ran high. The

---

[87] Brian Kissane, "Defending Democracy? The Legislative Response to Political Extremism in the Irish Free State, 1922–1939," *Irish Historical Studies* 34, no. 135 (2004): 326–352.

[88] Laura Cahillane, *Drafting the Irish Free State Constitution* (Manchester: Manchester Uni. Press, 2016), 91–135.

[89] Cahillane, *Drafting the Constitution*, 102.

[90] Mohr (2018), p.12.

execution of Republican prisoners, authorized under emergency powers by the new government, cast a shadow over the festive season.

According to Brian Farrell, Cork's citizens experienced a "split moral landscape" - where national loyalty, Catholic piety, and family life often came into conflict with military directives and ideological commitments.[91] Even within families, divisions ran deep: brothers fought on opposite sides, and Christmas dinner tables across Munster echoed with arguments instead of hymns.

Despite this, daily life carried on. Christmas pudding was served, choirs sang, and the Cork Butter Exchange buzzed with commerce. Churches offered Novena prayers for peace, and school nativity plays provided temporary refuge from the headlines. In this sense, Christmas in Cork 1922 was not a time of simple joy but of quiet resilience - a community insisting on tradition amidst national disarray.

In the years following the proclamation, Cork would remain central to the evolving Irish state. The civil war ended in 1923, but its political wounds lingered, especially in Cork's strong republican quarters. Over the next decade, debates about the Treaty, the Oath, and sovereignty would continue - culminating in Éamon de Valera's 1937 Constitution and the eventual declaration of the Republic of Ireland in 1949.

Yet 6 December 1922 remains pivotal. It was the first formal step in Ireland's political self-determination - a state born not in idealism but in negotiation, compromise, and bloodshed. For Cork, a city that had endured the worst of empire and resistance, it marked a threshold moment, even if many viewed it with scepticism or sorrow.

In writing about Christmas in Cork, we must acknowledge this complexity. The festive season that year was not just about candles in windows or holy days of obligation - it was a time of profound reckoning. The bells of Christmas 1922 rang out across a city changed forever, announcing both a child in the manger and a nation newly born, though far from fully free.

---

[91] M. Farrell, *Party Politics in a New Democracy: The Irish Free State, 1922–1937* (London: Palgrave, 2017), 33–58.

11

Conclusion

Christmas in County Cork: Faith, Frost, and Firelight

In the frosted stillness of a December dawn in nineteenth-century Cork, the bells of Shandon might be heard faintly tolling across the River Lee, their echo softened by morning mist and muffled footsteps. Holly wreaths adorned the doors of grand homes on Wellington Road and modest cottages in Blackpool alike. Market traders stirred on Cornmarket Street, boys hawked matches near the Coal Quay, and porters wheeled crates of oranges, hams, and firs imported from distant shores. There was joy and hardship, reverence and revelry, hunger and hospitality - all woven into the rich tapestry of a Cork Christmas.

This chapter explores the textures and tensions of Christmas in Cork between the 1840s and early 1900s - a period marked by extraordinary change, trauma, resilience, and cultural evolution. It was an era that witnessed the ravages of the Great Famine, waves of emigration, the rise of civic pride and commercial spectacle, deepening religious observance, and the emergence of nationalist sentiment. Through the lens of Christmas, we gain insight into a people negotiating the complexities of empire, modernity, memory, and identity - expressed through food, faith, music, market life, and mourning.

While Victorian ideals of Christmas - evergreens, crackers, department store displays - found their way into Cork via Britain, the city retained uniquely Irish traditions. The candle flickering in a window for Christ and absent kin, the midnight Mass echoing with Gaelic carols, the silence of an emigrant's chair at the hearth - these were emotionally charged rituals grounded in place and memory. In Cork, Christmas was not just a season of consumption or performance; it was one of remembrance, community, and resilience.

Cork's urban and geographic landscape shaped these experiences in vivid ways. The steep lanes of Shandon, the bustling stalls of the Coal Quay, the grandeur of St Fin Barre's Cathedral, and the carollers on Blarney Street offered contrasting yet connected worlds. The city was simultaneously a hub of transatlantic exchange and a close-knit community anchored in its own rhythms - parish life, market commerce, and intergenerational tradition.

This chapter does not treat Christmas as a static holiday but as a cultural prism refracting broader themes of Cork life: the shifting dynamics of poverty and charity, the spiritual hunger of a colonised people, the political meanings of celebration and absence, and the subtle resistance embedded in carols and cards. Drawing on newspaper advertisements, sermons, editorials, letters, oral traditions, and folk memory, we seek not only to uncover how Corkonians celebrated - but how they coped, resisted, hoped, and remembered.

Above all, this study embraces the tension between nostalgia and history. The romantic image of Victorian and Edwardian Christmases - snow on the eaves, laughter at the fire, roast goose on the table - is examined both as ideal and illusion. For many in Cork, Christmas meant not plenty but privation, not reunion, but absence and grief. Yet it was also a time when people gave from their scarcity, lit candles against the dark, and gathered in prayer, song, and defiant hope.

The pages that follow explore this cultural landscape in thematic depth: from the markets to the theatres, from the docks to the pews, from festive entertainments to famine shadows - different threads in Cork's Christmas story, drawing on archival sources and rich historical texture. Together, they offer a chorus of voices - working-class and elite, Catholic and Protestant, resident and emigrant - rising across a wintry city, warmed by firelight and fortified by faith.

From the mid-nineteenth century onward, Cork's festive season unfolded not only in homes and churches, but in streets, theatres, markets, and music halls - public spaces animated by colour, commerce, and collective cheer. Though the deeper religious tone of the season endured, urban life increasingly embraced spectacle and sociability as part of Christmas tradition. For both elites and working-class families, public entertainments became integral to how Christmas was celebrated, remembered, and enjoyed in the city.

The theatres of Cork offered a seasonal feast of performance. The Theatre Royal, located on George's Street (now Oliver Plunkett Street), was the city's premier venue for pantomimes, melodramas, and travelling troupes. During the Christmas period, pantomime reigned supreme. Plays such as *Cinderella*, *Harlequin and the Red Dwarf*, or *Jack and the Beanstalk* drew large crowds, blending fairy tale, slapstick comedy, moral allegory, and extravagant costuming. In its festive advertisements, the Theatre Royal promised "a production suitable for the entire family, adorned in glittering splendour and mirthful delight."[92]

---

[92] Cork Examiner, Friday 30 December 1870, p.2.

Attending the Christmas pantomime was a rite of passage for Cork children, many of whom had saved their pennies for weeks to afford a gallery seat. For wealthier families, theatre visits were part of an elaborate holiday circuit - dinner, promenade, and performance. Reports in the *Cork Constitution* describe crowds lining up "in laughter and glee" for tickets, with new gas lighting adding to the sense of festivity.[93]

Beyond the theatre, music halls and assembly rooms across the city offered seasonal concerts, sometimes for charity, sometimes for profit. The Athenaeum frequently hosted choral performances featuring schoolchildren, church choirs, and amateur orchestras. Programmes often included popular seasonal fare - Handel's *Messiah*, Irish airs such as *Silent O Moyle*, and English hymns like *While Shepherds Watched*. These concerts bridged the sacred and the secular, offering spiritual comfort while encouraging civic pride.

Markets, too, became seasonal spectacles. From the Coal Quay and the Grand Parade to St Patrick's Street, stalls overflowed with Christmas fayre, apples, puddings, geese, and greenery. A visitor to Cork in the 1890s might find lamp-lit shopfronts adorned with garlands. Christmas Eve was the highlight - "market night" - when stalls remained open late, the air filled with cries of traders and scents of pine, oranges, and cooked meats. Contemporary reports speak of "every hand bustling with parcels, every cart laden with turkeys, and every shop aglow with gaslight and gladness."[94]

Hawkers and tinkers arrived from surrounding countryside towns like Macroom, Middleton, and Bandon, swelling the city's population during the final days before Christmas. Horse-drawn carts rattled over the cobbles, filled with live poultry, turf, and seasonal wares. A visitor to Cork in 1875 would have seen geese tied by the legs and hung from shopfronts, or carts carrying meat toward English Market stalls. For many rural visitors, the Christmas cattle and horse fairs were not only commercial ventures but opportunities for news, drink, and reunion. These were lively affairs. The *Cork Constitution* recorded that "hundreds from the western baronies descended upon the city with calves, fowl, and turf in tow, returning with coin, cloth, or ribbons for their daughters."[95] Street performance was part of the sensory overload. Mummers and fiddlers paraded through the crowds. Carollers - especially children from Catholic schools - sang beneath shop windows and church porches, collecting coins for charity or school funds. According to one writer in the *Southern Reporter and Cork Commercial Courier*, "never is the city so alive as Christmas Eve,

---

[93] Cork Constitution, 2 January 1875, p.2.
[94] Southern Star, Saturday, 5 December 1896, p.1.
[95] Cork Constitution, 29 December 1868, p.1.

when even the poor man walks with pride, clutching a ham or goose, his children in tow and bells in the air."[96]

For the city's middle class, department stores and drapers such as Cash & Co., Arnott's, and Thompson's transformed shopping into seasonal theatre. Shop windows were dressed in scenes from Christmas stories, nativity displays, and imported luxury goods. An advertisement from December 1891 promoted "gloves, mufflers, perfumes, and Parisian novelties befitting the refined Irish home."[97] These displays fostered aspiration and nostalgia alike - offering glimpses into both Victorian domesticity and global modernity.

Meanwhile, more humble spectacles unfolded in the city's poorer districts. In the lanes of Barrack Street, Shandon, and the Marsh, community-organised raffles, soup kitchens, and children's pageants brought a quieter, more intimate form of celebration. Public houses and local grocers often donated food parcels, and street musicians performed seasonal ballads - *The Wexford Carol, Don Oíche Úd i mBeithil* - in the Irish language. These were no less theatrical for their informality, reinforcing the idea that joy was a communal resource, even where wealth was scarce.

Perhaps most striking was the way public spectacle and private piety coexisted. One could attend Midnight Mass at the North Cathedral, then wander down to the Coal Quay to hear fiddlers and buy a hot apple cake. The sacred and the sociable were not in conflict - they were complementary expressions of a shared cultural rhythm that made Christmas in Cork both exuberant and profoundly local. The festive entertainments of Cork - on stage, in market, or on street - were thus far more than distraction. They were moments of joy in a city often shadowed by economic difficulty, political unrest, and mass emigration. They offered ritual, repetition, and community at a time when many families felt fragmented. Through laughter, music, and light, Corkonians declared - against all odds and in their own accents - that the season would be marked with warmth, spectacle, and shared humanity.

Music and performance were at the very heart of Cork's Christmas celebrations in the nineteenth century. Whether in the grand surrounds of the city's theatres or on the flagstones of its market streets, the season was announced not only with bells and candles, but with voices raised in harmony. Formal concerts were hosted across Cork during Advent and the Twelve Days of Christmas. Mr McDowell's Great Room at the Imperial Hotel and the Athenaeum Theatre staged seasonal performances

---

[96] Southern Reporter and Cork Commercial Courier, 28 December 1852, p.2.
[97] Cork Constitution, 26 December 1891, p.5.

featuring choirs, soloists, and instrumental ensembles. Civic choirs performed Handel's *Messiah*, while school concerts offered charming renditions of *O Come, All Ye Faithful* and sentimental readings from Dickens and Moore. Notices in the *Cork Examiner* and *Cork Constitution* promoted these concerts as family events - opportunities for both devotion and enjoyment. One 1875 listing read: "The Gentlemen's Choral Society will present their annual Christmas recital, promising a programme of sacred and cheerful airs to lift the soul in the season's grace."[98]

Theatres were central to Cork's festive culture. Yet beyond pantomime, they also hosted seasonal operettas, folk dramas, and musical evenings that drew on both European and Irish traditions. Amateur societies performed *The Bohemian Girl*, *The Bells of Corneville*, and adaptations of *A Christmas Carol*. These performances often included local touches: actors in Cork accents, references to Patrick Street or Blarney, and jokes poking fun at English traditions. In this way, theatre became a medium not just of amusement but of cultural negotiation - where Irish identity played out in jest and lyric.

Music in the home was equally central. Even in modest houses, families gathered around hearths for an evening of singing, fiddling, and storytelling. Ballads such as *The Snowy Breasted Pearl*, *Eileen Aroon*, or the humorous *The Night Before Larry Was Stretched* were sung alongside seasonal favourites. Instruments like the tin whistle, concertina, and fiddle often accompanied these sessions, especially on Christmas Eve and St. Stephen's Night. In oral histories recorded in the early twentieth century, older Corkonians frequently recalled the warmth of these nights - when neighbours gathered with boiled puddings and strong porter, and music was passed down by ear and heart.

Church music took on particular significance during Midnight Mass and the Feast of the Epiphany. In the grand organ lofts of St Fin Barre's and Saints Peter and Paul's, choirs performed hymns in Latin and English, their harmonies resonating through Gothic naves lit by candle and gaslight. Choirboys rehearsed for weeks, and their voices - described in one 1860 account as "silver threads woven into prayer" - lifted hearts.[99]

For the city's Protestant congregations, Christmas music was equally rich. Carol services at St Anne's, Shandon and Holy Trinity were well attended. Hymns such as *O Come, Emmanuel* and *It Came Upon the Midnight Clear* were staples, often accompanied by readings from the Book of Common Prayer and passages from Isaiah and Luke. In contrast to

---

[98] *Cork Examiner*, Friday 24 December 1875, p.3.
[99] *Cork Constitution*, 27 December 1860, p.2.

Catholic rituals, these services emphasised word and song over pageantry - but both traditions shared a reverence for music's ability to draw communities together in sacred celebration.

Music also travelled. Emigrants sent home sheet music, harmonicas, and penny whistles in Christmas parcels. In turn, families wrote to sons and daughters in Boston, Liverpool, or Melbourne describing the carols sung at Mass or the "fine tunes played at Fr Crowley's school concert." One 1909 advertisement in the *Cork Examiner* invited families to send "a fiddle or flute as a fitting gift for the son far away, so that he too may hear the old songs at the blessed season."[100]

In sum, seasonal music in Cork was not a mere background to Christmas - it was its beating heart. From the dignity of cathedral choirs to the ragged charm of barefoot carolers, from the laughter in theatre balconies to the hush of a tin whistle at a kitchen fire, music wove Cork's Christmas together. It elevated the spirit, masked sorrow, honoured memory, and created shared joy across class, creed, and community.

The law, too, was present. Christmas markets required policing - not just to prevent pickpocketing or stall disputes, but to manage the great crowds. Occasionally, drunken fights broke out or street brawls disrupted trade. Reports from 1870 noted that "despite the cheer, the constabulary were twice called to break up inebriated gatherings outside public houses in Douglas Street and Paul Street."[101] Yet these incidents were often forgiven as part of the season's raucousness.

Importantly, market life mirrored broader economic conditions. In famine years or during trade depressions, stalls were fewer, prices dearer, and baskets lighter. During the harsh winter of 1846, the *Cork Constitution* reported 'a pitiful market, in which vendors of holly did more charity than trade, and many a stall bore no more than candle-stubs and dried bread.'[102]

Still, even in lean years, the market was a place of hope. A warm pie, a sprig of holly, or a hot potato bought from a street cart gave a sense of season. Children marvelled at shop windows even if they could not enter, and adults exchanged greetings and laughter, however strained. The markets allowed Cork's citizens to participate in the shared theatre of Christmas, regardless of wealth.

Cork's market squares at Christmas were not merely commercial hubs. They were stages for performance, venues for sociality, spaces of memory and class encounter. Whether one came to buy, to sing, to beg, or to be seen, the streets of Cork became democratic arenas of warmth,

---

[100] Cork Examiner, 22 December 1909, p.5.
[101] Cork Examiner, 30 December 1870, p.2.
[102] Cork Constitution, 23 December 1845, p.3.

light, and festivity. The market was, in essence, the city's open-air drawing room - a place where, in the season of darkness, Cork's people found communion in colour, noise, and shared tradition.

While the festive markets of Cork rang with cheer and commerce, another kind of Christmas tradition unfolded more quietly but no less powerfully in the parlours, chapels, and soup kitchens of the city: acts of charity. The spirit of giving, long entwined with both Catholic and Protestant understandings of the season, took tangible form in Cork through organised benevolence, spontaneous almsgiving, and the tireless work of religious and civic leaders. In a city shaped by poverty and inequality, philanthropy at Christmas offered both spiritual solace and practical relief.

From the 1840s onward, newspaper reports highlight Christmas as a key moment for charitable acts. One 1845 edition of the *Cork Examiner* noted: "The rich of our city have again shown themselves generous at this solemn time, and not a few tables in Blackpool and Blarney Street will enjoy warmth and meat through their donations."[103] These acts of giving were not mere performance; they were lifelines for thousands.

The Irish Famine (1845–1852) deepened the urgency of Christmas charity. While the famine's impact extended far beyond the city, Cork's urban poor swelled in numbers as people fled rural starvation. Soup kitchens multiplied. The Poor Law Guardians operated additional workhouse wards during the Christmas period. Religious leaders - most notably Archbishop Michael Slattery - issued pastoral letters urging both prayer and practical help. In a particularly moving 1847 Christmas appeal, Slattery called upon the faithful to "see in the Christ child the face of the hungry beggar at your door."

Even as the Famine raged, British official response remained sluggish. Exports of grain and livestock from Cork port continued unabated while thousands starved. The *Cork Constitution* reported on ships laden with butter bound for Liverpool even as local families queued for a ladle of broth. Attempts by Cork's local dignitaries - including Catholic clergy and liberal Protestant merchants - to raise the alarm in Parliament were often dismissed or delayed.

The contrast with Victorian London at Christmas was striking. In England, the mid-century saw the rise of sentimentalised Yuletide traditions: roast goose, gift-giving, parlour games, and snow-draped windows. Dickens's *A Christmas Carol* had captured the English imagination, fostering an image of redemption and hearthside joy. Yet in

---

[103] Cork Examiner, 29 December 1845, p.2.

Cork, families lit candles beside coffins, and children stared hungrily at shop windows filled with treats they would never taste.

Nonetheless, even amidst tragedy, philanthropy in Cork remained vibrant. The 1850s and 1860s saw the growth of charitable societies: the St Vincent de Paul Society, and the Protestant Orphan Society, all intensified activities in December. Parish bulletins called for food, clothing, and alms; local papers published lists of donors and gifts distributed. The work of John Arnott, a prominent Cork businessman and philanthropist, is particularly notable. Arnott personally hosted annual dinners for poor children in the Imperial Hotel's ballroom - an event described in 1875 as "the only feast these little ones may know, yet one they will carry in memory as a treasure of gladness" [104] By the late nineteenth century, larger public Christmas dinners became more common. Reports from 1896 and 1909 describe food being served to hundreds at St. Joseph's Asylum, the Good Shepherd Convent, and St Finbarr's Workhouse.

One advert from the *Southern Star* announced, 'a charity concert in aid of the poor children's Christmas dinner fund' with proceeds 'guaranteed to deliver meat, coal, and a sweet to every child on our list.'[105] Women played a central role in Christmas philanthropy. In both Catholic and Protestant circles, women organised food drives, sewed blankets, and delivered goods door-to-door. Many of these efforts went unrecorded, yet letters and memoirs attest to the persistence of female charitable labour, often carried out quietly through parishes, convents, and societies.

The press also shaped public engagement. Through editorial encouragement, donation lists, and accounts of festive generosity, the newspapers fostered a culture of visible, seasonally amplified charity. Philanthropy became part of the public ritual of Christmas - rooted in Christian obligation, civic pride, and a deep awareness of the city's inequalities.

Finally, it is worth noting how philanthropy blurred the line between giver and recipient. Many donors were only marginally better off than those they helped. Labourers shared bread with neighbours; widows sent coins to orphanages.

---

[104] George Pepper (ed), The Ancient Mode of Celebrating Christmas in Ireland, *The Irish Shield and Monthly Milesian*, vol. 1, 1829, pp.5-7.
[105] Southern Star, 5 December 1896, p.1.

THE STRINGENCY OF COERCION
THE INEFFECTIVENESS OF THE POOR LAW.

The Most Rev. Dr. SLATTERY, the spiritual head of the most afflicted portion of this unhappy country, has addressed the following pithy letter to the great statesman whose vigour and energy have been so oft glorified by the Premier, in his recent anti-Irish speeches. His Grace reminds the LORD LIEUTENANT of the indecent haste with which the Coercion Act is hurried into operation, while no care is taken for the lives of the poor, that are endangered by impending famine. The coercive measure is vigorously applied to the wretched country, while the Amended Poor Law, which was to prove such a blessing, which was to remodel society, and lay the foundation of a new order of things, is allowed "to remain almost a dead letter on the Statute Book."

The Whigs hurry a bill through Parliament for the preservation of the lives of the landlords, while they take no precaution to shield the multitudinous poor from a more deadly foe than the vengeful peasant who prowls abroad at night, or slays in the noon day. They have prevention and precaution in the one case; while in the other, they, with a singular piety, leave all to Providence. Police and military are summoned to guard the head of the landlord, and arms are torn from the hands of those whom bad laws have made desperate; but the poor are left to the deadly working of those iniquitous clauses, the ex-officio and quarter-acre provisions, by which the poor are bound neck and heels, and flung at the feet of a selfish and irresponsible class, to be trampled on, or starved, according to the promptings of their policy.

The Whigs reserve all their horrors and shudderings for crime; but they have no dread of starvation and pestilence-and yet these terrible scourges of our stricken land are again mowing down new victims, and raising up new earth-mounds, as monuments of their power.

Figure 18. *Cork Examiner*, 29 December 1847.

The Whigs reserve all their horrors and shudderings for crime; but they have no dread of starvation and pestilence-and yet these terrible scourges of our stricken land are again mowing down new victims, and raising up new earth-mounds, as monuments of their power.

Orrery and Kilmore are proclaimed and policed, while Skull is left to a renewal of last year's calamity. No later than this day did we read a letter from that locality, in which the writer gives the most painful instances of deaths from starvation. In fact, the work of death is steadily going on there, as in other parts of Ireland; yet the Whigs are only solicitous about the success of their Coercion Act. But hear what Archbishop Slattery says:-

Thurles, 26th December 1847.

MY LORD-You have been most prompt and vigorous in the exercise of the powers confided to you by the recent coercion act of the legislature. On the 20th instant it received the royal assent-on the 23rd your proclamation was issued to enforce its provisions; and this of course from a laudable anxiety for the protection of life, and the prevention of crime.

Would it not be well if your Excellency's vigilance was directed to another enactment, having also in view, as we were led to believe, the preservation of human life? I allude to the amended poor law for Ireland. This act was passed by the late parliament, but it still remains almost a dead letter on the statute book; for thousands of our poor people are daily famishing, and it is even reported that some have already perished of hunger.

Your Excellency has admitted in your answers to the memorial of the Catholic bishops that "the preservation of human life was the first and paramount duty of government." Are the lives of the rich and of the noble only to be protected, and shall it be always true that in Ireland "there is one law for the rich and another for the poor?"

I have the honour to remain, my Lord, your very obedient servant,

M. SLATTERY, Archbishop of Cashel.
To His Excellency the Earl of Clarendon.

A culture of mutual aid complemented institutional charity, reinforcing the idea that Christmas was not merely for the fortunate, but a season during which even the smallest act of kindness carried moral and communal weight.

In Cork, Christmas philanthropy did more than ease suffering. It offered moral structure, reinforced community ties, and allowed expressions of faith to take physical form. In a city both fractured and bound by poverty, the generosity of the season shone as one of its most luminous threads. Christmas was a profoundly spiritual season, marked not only by religious obligation but by genuine reverence, ritual preparation, and communal devotion. At a time when denominational identities deeply shaped everyday life, the city's religious celebrations of Christmas were both diverse and deeply felt. For Catholics and Protestants alike, it was a time of sacred observance, liturgical beauty, and reflection on the mysteries of the Incarnation amid the trials of life in a changing Ireland. For the city's Catholic majority, the climax of the season was Midnight Mass on Christmas Eve. In parishes across the city - from the towering North Cathedral to the humbler chapels of Shandon and Douglas - congregants gathered long before the hour. Streets were lined with flickering lanterns and candles placed in windows, a tradition said to welcome Mary and Joseph on their journey to Bethlehem. Entire families arrived in silence or quiet song, the chill night air broken only by the tolling of bells and whispered prayers.

An 1852 report from the *Southern Reporter* described the midnight liturgy at the North Cathedral as "a sight of awe and unity - farmers and weavers, widows and children kneeling beneath vaulted arches, their breath visible in the cold, their voices mingled in the ancient Latin rites."[106]

Confession and spiritual preparation were taken seriously in the weeks before Christmas. Catholic journals and pulpits reminded the faithful to "ready their hearts, not merely their hearths" for the Christ child. Missionaries and friars were often invited into parishes to preach Advent missions, offering both spiritual renewal and practical instruction. The Sacrament of Confession was central to this rhythm, especially during the famine years, when loss and guilt burdened many hearts.

On Christmas morning, families returned to Mass again - sometimes to a later liturgy, sometimes walking to rural chapels beyond the city. The Eucharist was understood not just as celebration but consolation. Many remembered those who had emigrated or died. The lighting of candles after Mass, particularly for absent family members, was

---

[106] Southern Reporter and Cork Commercial Courier, 28 December 1852, p.2.

both personal and communal. One 1847 description spoke of "a sea of wax and flame lit not merely for the infant Christ, but for the missing faces at table and fire"

For Cork's substantial Protestant community - comprising Anglican, Methodist, and Presbyterian congregations - Christmas was celebrated with equal solemnity, albeit in different liturgical tones. St. Anne's Church, Shandon, famed for its bells, hosted carol services from mid-December, with special readings and candlelit lessons held on Christmas Eve.

Scripture readings, drawn from Isaiah, Luke, and John, formed the heart of the service. Ministers preached on light in darkness, the gift of grace, and the bonds of community in Christ. A report from *The Cork Constitution* in 1860 noted that "the pews of Holy Trinity were filled not merely by its own congregation but by seekers from across the city, drawn to the quiet dignity of the liturgy and the splendour of its organ music."[107]

Choral music was particularly significant in Protestant services. Choirs performed ancient carols and new Victorian hymns alike. Anthems such as *O Come, All Ye Faithful, Lo! He Comes with Clouds Descending*, and *Angels from the Realms of Glory* rang through the stone walls, accompanied by pipe organs donated by benefactors. These services became social as well as spiritual events, with families greeting one another outside, often sharing mince pies or hot punch in adjacent parish halls.

Despite theological differences, both Catholic and Protestant communities in Cork shared certain festive rituals and symbols. The Christmas candle in the window - a deeply Irish tradition - was common across sectarian lines. The candle was a prayer in flame, a sign of hospitality to the divine and to the stranger.[108]

The exchange of Christmas cards and small gifts, initially a Protestant middle-class custom, spread across classes and confessions by the 1880s. Similarly, visits to the sick, charity for the poor, and communal meals for the lonely became shared expressions of the Christian message.

Moreover, emigration lent poignancy to religious observance. Many families attended Mass or service with a folded letter in their coat, sent from Boston, Liverpool, or Melbourne. These letters, often read aloud after worship, were part of the day's spiritual tapestry - bridging sea and soul in a season that valued connection.

Religious observance was not merely decorative; it provided moral structure, community coherence, and existential reassurance in a century

---

[107] Cork Constitution - Thursday 27 December 1860, p.2.
[108] George Pepper (1829), pp.5-7.

marked by famine, poverty, and loss. Clergy of all denominations used Christmas to reinforce social ethics, urge reconciliation, and offer hope. In the words of one 1869 sermon, "the cold of the stable is not far from us, nor is the exile's path unfamiliar - but Christ is born into this world, not apart from it. Here, too, he comes."[109]

In this way, spirituality and worship in Cork at Christmas were never isolated rituals - they were central threads in the fabric of civic and family life. Amid hardship and joy, the churches of Cork offered light, music, consolation, and sacred meaning - a reminder, for believer and doubter alike, that hope endures even in the deepest winter.

Of all the emotional threads running through a Corkonian Christmas in the nineteenth century, few were as powerful or as painful as the absence left by emigration. Cork was not just a city of celebration - it was a port of departure, the last place thousands of Irish men, women, and children saw before boarding ships bound for America, Canada, Australia, and beyond. The Christmas season, with its emphasis on home, family, and reunion, often heightened the sorrow of separation. It was, as one 1875 editorial phrased it, "a time when every empty chair at table whispers across the sea."[110]

Throughout the 1800s, Queenstown (now Cobh) in Cork Harbour was the chief emigration point for Ireland. In December, even as church bells rang and markets bustled, the harbour told another story. Ships prepared to depart even in winter months, carrying thousands into the unknown. Letters, packages, and remittances flowed both ways - but it was Christmas that sharpened the ache.

In newspapers like the *Cork Constitution* and *Southern Reporter*, it was common to find short notes in the classifieds: "A Merry Christmas to Patrick in Boston from his mother on Barrack Street," or "To my brother John, Australia - may your Christmas be blessed. We remember you at Mass." These snippets, easily overlooked, tell the real story of how emigration lived on in memory and ritual.

One December 1847 letter, published anonymously in the *Cork Examiner*, describes a mother lighting a candle in a window on Christmas Eve, "not just for the Holy Family, but for my Michael, whose boat left for Halifax last Michaelmas. May he see the light from Heaven where he cannot see ours."

Christmas correspondence was sacred. Letters from emigrants often arrived in December, posted weeks earlier, timed to reach home

---

[109] Southern Reporter and Cork Commercial Courier - Saturday 11 December 1869, p.2.
[110] Cork Examiner, 24 December 1875, p.3.

before the big day. They were read aloud after Mass or beside the hearth, sometimes several times. These letters might contain money, drawings from children, or descriptions of foreign Christmases - wintry in Montreal, sunlit in Melbourne.

One such letter from 1860, published in a local church bulletin, told of a Cork emigrant in New York: 'We had roast turkey and cranberry sauce, and I sang Silent Night for the first time in English... but it is not the same. I miss the sound of the bells from St Finbarr's and the candles in the windows.'

Families preserved these letters carefully. Some were re-read every Christmas for years. Others were copied into scrapbooks or prayer books, evidence that love had not been severed by oceans.

Though Christmas is popularly portrayed as a season of joy, for many in Cork it was laced with grief and longing. Songs like *The Exile's Return* or *The Emigrant's Lament* were performed in music halls and parlours alike. These were not just sentimental ballads - they were cultural acknowledgements of the wound that emigration inflicted on families and neighbourhoods.

Public rituals also reflected this sense of loss. Some Catholic churches encouraged families to light candles for absent kin during Christmas Mass. At Protestant services, ministers often referred to "our absent brethren abroad" in prayers. Emigration was not hidden - it was recognised, mourned, and integrated into the sacred rhythm of the holiday.

In the city's working-class neighbourhoods, particularly Blackpool, the Marsh, and Blarney Street, residents gathered to share news from abroad. Gifts sent home - cloth, tobacco, picture books - were displayed with pride. One oral history from the early twentieth century recalls "a tin soldier set from America arriving on Christmas Eve... and my mother crying because it came with a letter from Uncle Dan who had not written in three years."

While emigration brought sorrow, it also brought support. Remittances sent home by emigrants often funded Christmas dinners, clothing, or even church donations. An advertisement in the *Cork Examiner* in 1909 urged readers to "send a gift home: music box, shawl, or postal note - for Cork's sake, and Christ's."

Many of the city's philanthropic Christmas efforts, from children's feasts to soup kitchens, were funded in part by diaspora donations. Emigrants were not only mourned, they became patrons of Christmas in absentia. A common tradition across both Catholic and Protestant homes was to leave a place empty at the table on Christmas Day. Though nominally "for the stranger," in practice it often represented a missing family member - usually an emigrant. This chair, beside a flickering candle, became a domestic altar of memory. Some families placed an envelope or letter on the chair, others left a slice of cake or piece of ham, as if the absent might yet join the meal.

This tradition finds echoes in literature and folk memory across Cork. In a poem published in a Christmas edition of the *Southern Star*, a mother writes:

> We placed the cup where you once sat,
> And passed the jug as if you'd ask.
> The candle burned until the dawn -
> For you, though you are far and gone.

By the end of the nineteenth century, Cork's Christmas had become global. Parcels were posted from New York to the North Cathedral. Letters from Queensland were read at Douglas Street. The city's population remained ever-changing, ever-dispersed - but at Christmas, it tried to gather itself, even across oceans.

In this way, emigration did not sever Cork from its people. Rather, it stretched the city's emotional and spiritual geography across the world. Christmas became the thread that bound the home and the elsewhere, the present and the distant, the living and the long departed.

As the final candles of Christmas burned low in the parlours, chapels, and tenements of nineteenth-century Cork, they left behind more than wax and wick. They marked a time of year when memory grew warm against the cold, when grief and gladness coexisted by the firelight, and when a city divided by class, creed, and circumstance could, even if briefly, share in something sacred.

Throughout this chapter, we have explored the multifaceted nature of Christmas in Cork during a century of transformation. We've walked through bustling markets and narrow lanes where the scent of oranges mingled with coal smoke. We've entered theatres alive with song and laughter and stood in solemn church aisles echoing with Latin hymns and the soft murmur of candlelit prayer. We have witnessed the heartbreak of famine and emigration, the generosity of charitable kitchens, and the resilience of families who, year after year, lit candles for the absent, the lost, and the divine.

Christmas in Cork during this period was not merely a holiday; it was a cultural mirror, reflecting the city's joys and sorrows, its values and tensions. It was a festival layered with religious devotion, political undercurrents, social ritual, and emotional complexity. While English Victorian traditions filtered into Cork through empire and trade, the city retained - and reimagined - its own way of celebrating: one rooted in Irish language, Catholic piety, Protestant song, communal resilience, and deep familial longing.

As we have seen, even during the bleakest moments of the Great Famine, Corkonians lit candles and sang carols, not as a distraction, but as quiet acts of defiance and dignity. They celebrated Mass, staged pantomimes, and held onto traditions in times of grief. Emigration may have emptied homes, but it never fully silenced them - Christmas letters, parcels, and prayers bridged continents with messages of memory and love.

In reading the advertisements, editorials, sermons, and letters from this era, we gain more than historical detail. We encounter a deeply human Christmas: fraught with contradictions, rich in symbolism, animated by hope. We hear voices - of butchers and bakers, bishops and beggars - each contributing to a uniquely Corkonian carol of the season.

To understand Christmas in Cork in the Victorian and Edwardian eras is to understand a city in flux: coping with colonial pressures, reshaping its identity, and preserving its soul. The holiday provided a ritualised space where that soul could be expressed - in music, food, worship, market laughter, or the flicker of a single candle in a tenement window.

The memory of that Christmas lives on. It can still be heard in the echo of the Shandon bells, in the stories passed down through generations, and in the silent spaces we hold in our own celebrations - for those who are gone, those who are far, and those whose hopes remain lit by a flame that once flickered in the streets of Cork.

Bibliography

Peter Berresford Ellis, *Hell or Connaught! The Cromwellian Colonisation of Ireland* (Belfast: Blackstaff, 1985).

Ciaran Brady, *The Chief Governors: The Rise and Fall of Reform Government in Tudor Ireland, 1536–1588* (Cambridge: Cambridge University Press, 1994).

Laura Cahillane, *Drafting the Irish Free State Constitution* (Manchester: Manchester Uni. Press, 2016).

Nicholas Canny, *Making Ireland British, 1580–1650* (Oxford: Oxford University Press, 2001).

Cork Constitution

Cork Examiner

David Dickson, *Old World Colony: Cork and South Munster 1630–1830* (Cork: Cork University Press, 1947).

Ciarán O'Driscoll, "The Cork Butter Market, 1700–1800," *Irish Economic and Social History* 18 (1991), 31-49.

Steven G. Ellis, *Tudor Ireland: Crown, Community and the Conflict of Cultures* (London: Longman, 1998).

M. Farrell, *Party Politics in a New Democracy: The Irish Free State, 1922–1937* (London: Palgrave, 2017).

Cyril Falls, *Elizabeth's Irish Wars* (Syracuse: Syracuse University Press, 1996).

David Gwynn, *The Irish Free State, 1922–1927* (Dublin: Talbot Press, 1928).

Godfrey Higgins, The Celtic Druid (London: Hunter, 1827).

John Hobson Matthews, "Notes and Queries," 8th series, vol. 11, January–June 1897, 54.

Brian Kissane, "Defending Democracy? The Legislative Response to Political Extremism in the Irish Free State, 1922–1939," *Irish Historical Studies* 34, no. 135 (2004): 326–352.

Pádraig Lenihan, *Consolidating Conquest: Ireland 1603–1727* (London: Routledge, 2001).

Margaret MacCurtain and Donnchadh Ó Corráin, eds., *Women in Early Modern Ireland* (Dublin: Arlen, 1978).

T. F. McCarthy, "Markets and Trade in Seventeenth-Century Cork," *Journal of Munster Studies* 9, no. 2 (1998), 22-35.

James McCavitt, *The Flight of the Earls* (Dublin: Gill & Macmillan, 2002).

John McGurk, *Sir Henry Docwra, 1564–1631: Derry's Second Founder* (Dublin: Four Courts Press, 1997).

Thomas Mohr, "Law and the Foundation of the Irish State on 6 December 1922," *Irish Jurist* 60 (2018): 1-22.

Hiram Morgan, *Tyrone's Rebellion: The Outbreak of the Nine Years War in Tudor Ireland* (Woodbridge: Boydell, 1993).

Michael O'Neill, *Provisioning the Empire: Irish Ports and Global Trade, 1650–1750* (Manchester: Manchester University Press, 2014).

J.H. O'Neill, "The Battle of Kinsale," *Irish Historical Studies* 6, no. 21 (1948): 23–42.

George Pepper (ed), The Ancient Mode of Celebrating Christmas in Ireland, *The Irish Shield and Monthly Milesian*, vol. 1, 1829, .5-7.

Joseph Sanderson, *Story of St Patrick* (New York: Ketcham, 1895).

Southern Reporter and Cork Commercial Courier

Southern Star

Index

A

Advent, 98, 125, 164, 169, 176
Agharinagh, 74
Ahadallane, 121
Aherla, 64
Ahernal, 68
All Souls, 12, 78
Allihies, 66
altar, 11, 20, 24, 74, 77, 91, 94, 128, 142, 145, 180
America, 21, 34, 155, 178, 179
An Doineann, 27, 36, 41
angels, 92
Anglo-Irish gentry, 15
Anglo-Irish Treaty, 163
Annagannihy, 83
Araglin, 81
Archbishop Michael Slattery, 172
Ardkitt West, 133
Arnott's, 169
Athenaeum Theatre, 169
Atlantic, 23, 36, 44, 48, 146, 147, 150
Atlantic Ocean, 36
Australia, 178

B

Baile 'nChalaidh, 34
Ball Alley, 64
Ballacummer Bridge, 90
Ballinacubby Creek, 62, 64
Ballineen, 90
Ballinglanna, 127, 128, 134, 137
Ballybane West, 130
Ballycotton, 44, 48, 49, 52, 55, 56, 57, 58
Ballydehob, 118, 125, 127, 130, 132, 137
Ballydesmond, 73
Ballydonegan, 66
Ballyhea, 95, 96, 112, 124
Ballyvahallig Crossroads, 90
Bandon, 67, 79, 80, 117, 168
Bandon river, 67
Banteer, 123
Bantry, 14, 15, 16, 37, 38, 59, 72, 119, 155, 161, 162
Bantry Bay, 155, 159, *See* Bantry
Bantry House, 14, 15, 16
Barrack Street, 22, 23, 169, 178
Battle of Kinsale, 157
bean-a-tí, 27, 31
Beara, 16

beeswax, 11, 14, 22
bell, 12, 16, 19, 74, 85, 108, 170
Bere Island, 95, 105, 125
Berrings, 74, 110, 111
best:, 62
Bethlehem, 12, 78, 82, 99, 107, 176
Bird Island, 35, 132
Black and Tans, 73
Blackpool, 24, 166, 172, 179
blackthorn, 78, 82
Blarney Street, 166, 172, 179
Blind Gate, 64
block na Nodlag, 99
boat, 34, 36, 37, 42, 54, 56, 68, 89, 108, 147, 178
Boherboy, 127, 128, 134, 137
Boston, 11, 19, 23, 171, 177, 178
Brandy Hall, 105, 124
bread, 28, 31, 43, 63, 75, 93, 108, 135, 138, 171, 173
Bristol, 48, 49
Britain, 2, 18, 48, 140, 149, 155, 166
British Empire, 45
British Navy, 116
Butter Exchange, 149, 150, 165

C

cairns, 140
calendar, 12, 56, 124, 129
Canada, 35, 164, 178
candle, 11, 12, 14, 16, 18, 19, 20, 22, 23, 24, 27, 28, 30, 31, 32, 41, 43, 59, 62, 63, 75, 78, 89, 92, 95, 98, 99, 100, 105, 107, 110, 124, 126, 139, 159, 166, 170, 171, 177, 178, 180, 181
candlelight, 14, 16, 19, 21, 61, 74, 85, 157
Carbery Island, 132
cargo, 33, 35, 48, 49, 59
Carn. *See* Currane
carol, 12, 22, 144, 177, 181
carollers. *See* Carol
Carrigaline, 110, 124
Carrig-an-Aifrinn, 74
Carrigfadtha hill, 119
Cash & Co., 20, 21, 22, 169
Castle Donovan:, 117
Castlewrixon, 112
Cathedral, 108, 169, 176, 180
Catholic, 11, 16, 21, 22, 66, 68, 77, 78, 79, 82, 95, 124, 150, 158, 165, 167, 168, 171, 172, 173, 176, 177, 179, 181
chieftain, 144, 145

184

children, 11, 14, 18, 20, 21, 30, 43, 62, 70, 73, 74, 80, 81, 92, 96, 98, 100, 101, 105, 108, 110, 112, 122, 123, 127, 131, 138, 163, 168, 169, 173, 176, 178, 179
chimney, 69, 75, 84
Christ, 11, 12, 15, 16, 19, 24, 59, 78, 79, 80, 81, 92, 100, 124, 141, 145, 159, 166, 172, 176, 177, 178, 179
Christ child, 11, 24, 59, 124, 140, 159, 172, 176
Christmas, 1, 11, 12, 14, 15, 16, 18, 19, 20, 21, 22, 23, 24, 27, 28, 29, 30, 31, 32, 33, 34, 35, 36, 37, 38, 41, 42, 43, 44, 45, 48, 49, 52, 54, 55, 56, 57, 58, 59, 60, 61, 62, 64, 66, 67, 68, 71, 72, 73, 74, 75, 77, 78, 79, 80, 81, 82, 84, 85, 86, 87, 88, 89, 92, 93, 94, 95, 96, 97, 98, 99, 100, 101, 105, 106, 107, 110, 111, 112, 114, 115, 116, 117, 118, 119, 120, 122, 124, 125, 127, 130, 131, 137, 140, 141, 143, 144, 145, 149, 152, 155, 157, 158, 159, 163, 164, 165, 166, 167, 168, 169, 170, 171, 172, 173, 176, 177, 178, 179, 180, 181, 183
Christmas cake, 100
Christmas Day, 27, 32, 34, 45, 52, 54, 56, 62, 79, 80, 81, 93, 95, 96, 100, 106, 107, 110, 114, 116, 117, 119, 120, 140, 141, 155, 179
Christmas eve, 33, 100, 105, 143, 144
Christmas Shipwrecks, 35
Christmastide, 11
church, 11, 12, 28, 52, 58, 61, 64, 93, 119, 126, 144, 145, 150, 168, 178, 179, 180
Cill Mhichíl, 34
Civil War, 163
Clashadoo, 35
Cloan, 36
Clonakilty, 90, 119
Cnoc an Fiolar, 62, 66
Cnoc Fuara, 66
Coachford, 121
Coal Quay, 21, 166, 168, 169
Cobh, 59, 108, 178
colonisation, 11
community, 12, 29, 41, 42, 44, 54, 61, 62, 63, 74, 95, 97, 124, 125, 128, 137, 139, 147, 150, 165, 166, 169, 171, 176, 177
concertina, 170
Conchubhair, 101
Conna, 113
Connach, 99
Coom, 66
Coomdelame, 38
Corelli, 150

Cork, 14, 15, 18, 20, 21, 22, 23, 24, 27, 32, 35, 37, 38, 42, 44, 45, 48, 49, 52, 54, 55, 56, 57, 58, 59, 60, 66, 79, 80, 82, 85, 89, 95, 96, 97, 98, 100, 101, 110, 119, 120, 121, 124, 125, 126, 127, 128, 129, 131, 132, 137, 138, 139, 146, 147, 149, 150, 152, 154, 155, 158, 159, 163, 164, 165, 166, 167, 168, 169, 170, 171, 172, 173, 176, 177, 178, 179, 180, 181, 182, 183
Cork Constitution, 21, 168, 169, 170, 171, 172, 177, 178, 182
Cork Examiner, 18, 164, 167, 170, 171, 172, 178, 179, 182
Cork Harbour, 48, 54, 55, 56, 178
Cornmarket Street, 166
cottage, 11, 14, 16, 27, 30
County Cork, 1, 24, 29, 44, 95, 124, 155, 157, 158, 166
cow, 14, 82, 88, 92
Creagh, 33
cream, 14, 23
cromlechs, 140
Cromwell, 86
Crosshaven, 89
Currane, 67

D

dancing, 87, 97, 125
darkness, 12, 16, 19, 24, 27, 28, 41, 42, 43, 44, 62, 80, 143, 159, 172, 177
dawn, 11, 71, 79, 96, 163, 166, 180
Dearg Daol, 83, 93
decorations, 30, 42, 95, 110
department store, 20, 22, 166
Derreennalomane, 132
Derrinagree, 102
Derrycreeveen, 105, 106
Derryduff, 133
Dickens, 24, 170, 172
disaster, 35, 48, 49, 54, 58, 138
DNA, 24
donkey, 82, 93
Donnachadh Ua Laoghaire, 37
Douglas, 171, 176, 180
Douglas Street, 171, 180
Dr Orr, 64
Drimoleague, 11, 95, 115, 116, 117
Drinagh, 85, 119
Drishane, 102, 132
Droumousta, 116
Dublin, 2, 18, 21, 49, 54, 118, 121, 157, 158, 159, 163, 182
Dunbeacon, 127, 132
Dunboy, 66

185

dungeon, 84
Dunmanus, 35
Dunmanus Bay, 132
Dursey, 34

E

eagles, 62, 66
Earls of Bantry. *See* Bantry
electric lights, 42, 155
emigrant, 20, 166, 167, 179, 180
Empire:, 149, 183
Enniskean, 128, 133
Epiphany, 32, 96, 140, 170
Eucharist, 11, 176
exile, 11, 23, 24, 44, 178

F

fairies, 77, 78, 88, 92, 93, 94
faith, 19, 22, 58, 59, 61, 62, 74, 75, 77, 78, 79, 92, 93, 94, 95, 124, 126, 143, 166, 167, 176
famine, 11, 12, 14, 15, 18, 19, 22, 23, 55, 59, 78, 166, 167, 171, 172, 176, 178, 180, 181
Fermoy, 136, 137
fertility customs, 124
fiddle, 102, 104, 125, 170, 171
Finnaha, 66
fire, 11, 12, 14, 16, 23, 30, 33, 68, 87, 92, 96, 99, 100, 101, 105, 112, 123, 126, 135, 157, 158, 167, 171, 177
First Foot, 113
fisherman, 64, 134
fishermen, 36, 54, 57
flood, 42, 130, 131
fog, 21, 27, 37, 41, 54, 57, 59, 89
folklorist, 140
Fountainstown, 89
Fr Mac Namara, 64, 65
Fr Nicholas O'Connor, 19
Friars Street, 64
frost, 11, 12, 42, 74, 104, 106, 133, 136, 158

G

gale, 36, 52, 54, 56, 130
Galway, 19, 49, 145
garlands, 12, 14, 144, 168
gathered:, 138
Geese, 119, 125
George's Street. *See* Oliver Plunkett Street
ghost, 18, 42, 78, 79, 81, 84, 87, 92, 93

Glan, 114, 115
Glanmore, 87
Glantane, 120, 124
Glennamucklagh East, 86
Gneeveguilla, 73
Good People, 78, 88, 93
goose. *See* geese
Grand Parade, 168
Graveyard, 33
Great Famine. *See* Famine
Great Storm of 1839, 127
Green-coat Hospital, 149
grief, 15, 16, 19, 23, 27, 41, 43, 52, 56, 58, 59, 77, 78, 93, 167, 179, 180, 181
guncotton, 35

H

hake, 62, 65, 101
Hammond's Marsh, 146, 149
Handel, 150, 168
Handel's Messiah, 168, 170
harmonicas, 21, 171
Harry Casey, 70
Harvest of the Geese, 119
hearth, 14, 18, 20, 21, 22, 23, 52, 61, 74, 92, 94, 95, 125, 144, 157, 166, 179
hides, 48, 147, 149
holly, 14, 20, 21, 24, 31, 32, 67, 79, 80, 81, 82, 93, 95, 96, 98, 99, 100, 102, 104, 105, 106, 107, 110, 112, 114, 115, 118, 120, 124, 144, 145, 171
Holly Green, 116, 117
Hollyhill, 72
Holy Communion, 81, 110
Holy Family, 11, 20, 27, 28, 31, 41, 42, 43, 45, 57, 58, 62, 78, 82, 83, 93, 178
holy water, 68, 99
horse, 66, 69, 75, 83, 86, 90, 121, 168
hunger, 14, 16, 19, 20, 62, 70, 71, 74, 75, 108, 132, 157, 166, 167
hymns, 11, 16, 165, 168, 170, 177, 180

I

Imperial Hotel, 169, 173
Inchiclogh, 72
Inchidaly, 123
Indian meal gruel, 138
Innisbeg, 33
Ireland, 1, 11, 12, 15, 18, 21, 23, 24, 28, 29, 35, 44, 45, 48, 55, 56, 57, 75, 77, 78, 92, 93, 94, 95, 98, 113, 121, 127, 129, 137, 140, 142, 144, 145, 146, 149, 157, 158,

159, 163, 164, 165, 173, 176, 178, 182, 183
Irish Folklore Commission, 29
Irish Free State, 163, 164, 165, 182
Islandbrack, 136
ivy, 14, 80, 81, 82, 93, 95, 98, 100, 101, 102, 106, 110, 112, 115, 118, 144

J

Jack Murphy, 72
Joan Roaster, 62, 65, 74
Joseph, 23, 96, 124, 173, 176, 183

K

Keale North, 102, 125
Kerry, 66, 70, 111, 144
kettle, 12, 96, 99, 102, 104, 110, 112, 115, 130, 139
Kilaginish, 104, 124
Kilcasken, 67
Kilcronat, 107
Killarney, 73, 122
Kilmeen, 33
Kilnacloona, 64
Kilnamartyra, 99
Kilshinahan, 68
Kilvilogue, 28, 33, 42
Kilworth, 81
King George V, 163, 164
Kinneigh, 67
Kinsale, 44, 49, 52, 55, 56, 57, 59, 64, 68, 90, 157, 158, 159, 183
Knockaneady, 33, 67
Knocknagree, 122, 124
Knockskagh, 90

L

landlord, 38, 64
Latin, 12, 170, 176, 180
Lehana, 116
Letter, 132
light, 11, 12, 14, 15, 16, 18, 19, 20, 23, 24, 27, 28, 32, 33, 41, 42, 43, 44, 58, 62, 75, 93, 94, 100, 111, 113, 124, 126, 132, 141, 159, 160, 169, 172, 177, 178, 179
Limerick, 49, 121, 149
Liscarroll, 96, 106, 107
Little Christmas, 32, 101, 125
Liverpool, 19, 49, 171, 172, 177
Lombardstown, 120

London, 11, 18, 21, 22, 24, 48, 141, 142, 158, 163, 165, 172, 182
Lord Kinsale, 64

M

Má Gun, 74
Macroom, 95, 99, 168
Mallow, 121
Market House, 147
Market Lane, 65
Mary, 23, 74, 77, 96, 98, 100, 124, 132, 176
Maryfield, 84
Mass, 12, 16, 18, 19, 23, 42, 45, 59, 61, 62, 64, 66, 68, 74, 75, 78, 79, 80, 81, 85, 86, 92, 93, 94, 98, 110, 119, 125, 128, 138, 155, 166, 169, 171, 176, 177, 178, 179, 181
McGee, 143
Mealagh, 117
Meelin, 86, 104, 119
Meenies:, 117
Melbourne, 171, 177, 179
Michaelmas, 96, 119, 125, 149, 178
Middleton, 168
Midnight Mass, 170, *See* Mass
milking, 14
Millstreet, 80
Minane, 89
mist, 11, 12, 16, 20, 27, 35, 89, 160, 166
mistletoe, 21, 81, 110, 140, 141, 142, 143, 144
Mizen Head, 27, 35
money, 30, 64, 70, 80, 96, 100, 102, 104, 106, 107, 110, 113, 114, 115, 179
Moore, 16, 68, 87, 170
mouth organ, 102, 104, 125
Mr McDowell's Great Room, 169
Muddy Lane, 64
Munster, 147, 165, 182
murder, 38, 160
music, 12, 15, 19, 20, 21, 63, 96, 104, 124, 125, 145, 154, 155, 166, 167, 168, 169, 170, 171, 177, 178, 179, 181
musical instrument, 104
Muskerry, 149

N

Nantes, 48
nativity, 18, 20, 159, 165, 169
navigation, 44
New Tipperary, 121
New Year's Day, 111, 113, 118, 121
New York, 48, 144, 179, 180, 183

187

Newmarket, 86, 119, 131
Night of the Big Wind. *See* Great Storm of 1839
North Cathedral, 176
North Cork:, 24
North Island, 146
Nyhan, 87

O

O'Sullivan Beares, 66
Oíche na Gaoithe Móire. *See* Great Storm of 1839
Oileán Aolbhach, 27, 34
Old Court, 33
Old Head of Kinsale, 44
Oliver Plunkett Street, 167
Opera House, 164
Owen Hill:, 117
Oxford:, 158, 182
Oyster Haven, 90

P

Pana. *See* Patrick Street
Pancake Night. *See* Shrove Tuesday
pantomimes, 164, 167, 181
parish, 12, 16, 22, 48, 61, 73, 105, 110, 125, 166, 177
parlour games, 16, 172
Passage, 152
Patrick Street, 20, 170
Paul Street, 171
Penal Times, 74, 86
penance, 79, 92
penny whistles, 171
persecution, 27
plum pudding, 81
Poll an Bhitheamhnaigh, 62, 67
Poor Law Guardians, 18, 172
potatoes, 18, 96, 99, 100, 101, 135, 138
Poteen Still, 117
poverty, 18, 19, 28, 70, 78, 79, 167, 172, 176, 178
prayer, 11, 15, 16, 19, 43, 77, 91, 93, 95, 126, 128, 144, 167, 170, 172, 177, 179, 180
Presentation Convent, 21
priest, 12, 18, 19, 59, 62, 65, 68, 74, 75, 78, 79, 80, 86, 89, 90, 91, 93, 94, 128, 138, 143, 144
priest-hunters, 62
Protestant Orphan Society, 173
pudding, 14, 18, 24, 95, 107, 112, 125, 165
Puxley, 66

Q

Queensland, 180
Queenstown. *See* Cóbh

R

railways, 152, 155
Rathcoola West, 98
Red Abbey, 147, 149
Reflections, 41, 74, 124
Regatta, 108
Ringabella, 54, 55, 56, 89
River Ilen, 33
River Lee, 146, 166
Riverstick, 100, 124
Riverstown House, 87
Roaring water, 119
Roberts Cove, 48
robin, 78, 79, 82, 92
Rome, 74, 142, 145
Rotterdam, 48
Royal Navy, 45, 52, 149

S

sacred groves, 140
saints, 78, 92
Saints Peter and Paul's, 170
Sand Key, 146, 147, 149
Santa Claus, 80, 81, 98, 112, 163
Scarteen, 86
schools, 64, 93, 168
Schull, 89
sea, 27, 28, 34, 36, 42, 44, 45, 48, 49, 52, 54, 56, 57, 58, 59, 89, 177, 178
Seán a' Gabha, 89
seine, 36
Shanballyshane, 99
Shandon, 166, 169, 170, 176, 177, 181
shipwrecks, 27, 35, 41, 44, 45, 52, 56, 58, 59, 61, 62
Shrove Tuesday, 111, 125, 133
Skeaf, 69
Skellig Rock, 111
Skibbereen, 15, 16, 18, 19, 20, 59, 117
sleet, 16, 130
sloop, 48, 52, 54
snow, 16, 20, 23, 66, 69, 87, 104, 106, 127, 128, 130, 132, 133, 134, 135, 136, 137, 138, 167, 172
snowploughs, 129
snowstorm, 132, 134, 135, 136, 138, *See* snow

sour milk, 135, 138
South Island, 146
South Main Street, 147
Southampton, 48
Southern Reporter, 168, 169, 176, 178, 183
Southern Star, 168, 173, 180, 184
Spanish Army, 66
St Burceart, 119
St Fin Barre's, 166, 170
St Patrick's Street, 168
St Stephen's Day, 96, 102
St Vincent de Paul Society, 173
Sthickeen, 119
stockfish, 95, 100, 125
storm, 27, 28, 34, 35, 36, 41, 48, 49, 52, 54, 56, 57, 58, 59, 127, 128, 129, 130, 131, 132, 134, 137, 138, 139, 158, 159, 160
storytelling, 41, 61, 96, 125, 138, 170
superstition, 28, 77, 78, 81, 92, 93, 94, 141
swimming, 89

T

tallow, 48, 147
taper, 11
Telegraphy, 155
Temple Brigid, 89
thatch, 11
the Boyd. *See* Shipwrecks
the Britannia, 49, 54
the Chalice Tree, 86, 92
the Charlotte. *See* Shipwrecks
the Dispatch. *See* Shipwrecks
the Friendship. *See* Shipwrecks
The Gentlemen's Choral Society, 170
the Hope. *See* Shipwrecks
the Iberia, 27
The Invasion, 159, 160
the John of Barnstable, 48
the Nancy. *See* Shipwrecks
the Oswego, 48
The Peggy. *See* Shipwrecks
the Pembroke, 48
The Philadelphia, 49, *See* Shipwrecks
The Rio, 27, 34, 41
The Squire, 48
the Two Friends. *See* Shipwrecks
the Union, 49
the Unity, 48
The Wexford Carol, 21, 169
theatre, 20, 153, 154, 168, 169, 170, 171

Theatre Royal, 167
theology, 13, 77, 140
Thompson's, 169
Timothy Cadogan, 28, 38, 42
tin whistle, 170, 171
tobacco, 48, 179
Tomás na Hoola, 89
Tráigh An Phéarla, 36
transformation:, 146
Tullylease, 119
turkey, 81, 95, 100, 101, 107, 110, 112, 125, 179
turnip, 27, 31, 32, 42, 61

V

ventriloquist, 65
vigil, 11
Virginia, 48

W

War of Independence, 163
wassail bowl, 144, 145
Wellington Road, 24, 166
well-water, 14
West Cork, 89, 149, 163
Whiddy, 37
Whiskey, 72
William Birde, 38
William O Shea, 89
wind, 23, 24, 37, 57, 58, 62, 82, 92, 127, 128, 130, 134, 137, 162
winter, 18, 27, 28, 42, 44, 45, 52, 56, 57, 78, 81, 90, 91, 127, 128, 129, 137, 138, 139, 142, 158, 171, 178
Women's Christmas, 32, 96, 111
Wordsworth, 16
wreck, 33, 35, 48, 49, 52, 54, 55, 56, 58, 59, 71
Wren, 96, 100, 104, 107, 113, 114, 120, 124
Wren Boys, 96, 114
Wren song, 96

Y

Youghal, 48, 49, 54, 55, 57, 58
Yule logs, 97

www.ingramcontent.com/pod-product-compliance
Lightning Source LLC
Chambersburg PA
CBHW052030070526
44584CB00016B/1986